The Dirtbag's Guide to Life

Eternal Truth for Hiker Trash, Ski Bums, and Vagabonds

Tim Mathis

The Dirtbag's Guide to Life: Eternal Truth for Hiker Trash, Ski Bums, and Vagabonds

CONTENTS

Acknowledgements

Special thanks to my wife Angel, my editor Rob "Danger Muffin" Zimmerman, and Megan Myers, who designed the art for this project. You're all a bunch of freaking dirtbags.

To everyone - thank you so much for reading the print edition of this book!

For a note on how to use this book as a resource, I've referenced dozens of websites and organizations throughout the text. In order to make it easy to learn more, I've done my best to include them (along with a bunch of other useful links) in the appendix at the end.

Dear Reader,

You might not consider yourself a dirtbag, and that's okay. But I want to make something clear from the start: if you *do*, I want to assure you that you don't need to feel threatened around me.

I see the way they look at you when you walk in the room (because you stink). I know the pain you feel when your friends don't invite you over anymore (because they can't get that stain you left out of their couch). I know how frustrating it is that your parents insist on you paying rent (because you're 34). I know because I've walked in your shoes.

They assume that you're just some loser that doesn't want a job, or that you're going to shoplift their Cheetos because you still have a little orange dust on your lip. They assume that you just don't know what the hell you're doing with your life.

But they don't understand that you're the modern Shackleton, the woke Ed Abbey. And without people like you, no one would know what the top of a mountain looks like. They would have to skip their day hikes because there would be no trails. Oprah wouldn't be so inspired because Reese Witherspoon would have to go "Wild" on a sidewalk in Des Moines, and "Endless Summer" would just be about a sunburned Midwesterner at the Holiday Inn in Destin. The world would have no underwater photography, no X Games, and would care not a whit for fresh pow. Hell, without you no American kid would have bike toured around Europe, and none of your peers would know the possibilities of single payer healthcare or legalized pot.

What they see as signs of indigence are actually your badges of honor, your irrefutable evidence of commitment to the cause. If you live in your van, it's because there are no apartments to rent at the base of the Dawn Wall. If your clothes are filthy, it's because there are no laundry machines where you spend your afternoons, 30 miles from the nearest trailhead. And if you eat Meow Mix, it's because surfing doesn't pay, and that stuff's cheaper than people food.

You're keeping the spirit of the Dharma Bums alive: Grandma Gatewood and Yvon Chouinard, Wendell Berry and John Mother F'n Muir. Your work's born the fruit of Greenpeace, Patagonia, and the National Park System. And those trust fund #vanlifers and their beautiful, sepia-filtered Instagram feeds - their art is imitating your life.

You've turned their pejorative into a term of endearment. You've taken the Valley Uprising and turned it into a revolution. You've taken outdoor recreation and made it Universal Truth.

You're the modern day explorer, and you're bound to change the world.

And this manifesto is dedicated to you, the highest proof distillation of modern adventure.

DIRTBAG:

"A person who is committed to a given (usually extreme) lifestyle to the point of abandoning employment and other societal norms in order to pursue said lifestyle. Dirtbags can be distinguished from hippies by the fact that dirtbags have a specific reason for their living communaly (sic) and generally non-hygenically (sic); dirtbags are seeking to spend all of their moments pursuing their lifestyle.

The best examles (sic) of dirtbags and dirtbagging are the communities of climbers that can be found in any of the major climbing areas of North America--Squamish, BC; Yosemite, CA; Joshua Tree, CA; etc.

#hippy#bum#climber#surfer#backpacker#hitchhiker"

by Shay (dirtbag wannabe) August 17, 2007

Urban Dictionary

INTRODUCTION

Hey people, welcome to the Dirtbag's Guide to Life, your manual for living an adventure-filled life on the cheap. What you're getting into, at heart, is a manifesto outlining the philosophy that adventure is for everyone - or at least everyone who wants it - and that the good life can be had even for those of you with no inheritance, no skills, and no prospects. The best things in life are free, and the shit that's not you can buy at the thrift store. This is a book about how and why.

I'm Tim, and I'm writing this as someone who's been doing this stuff myself, in some capacity or another, for a couple of decades now. My wife and I are immersed in dirtbaggery personally as hikers, travelers, runners, and paddlers, but also professionally as co-owners of a business called *Boldly Went* that congeals the wisdom of the dirtbag masses through live storytelling events, interviews, and a couple of different podcasts.

My goal here is to distill as much useful information as I can, because I want to give you a handbook for living "the good life" of fun and adventure even if you can't (or prefer not to) spend a ton of money.

Before we get too far into any of that though, let's talk a bit about how we all got here.

Who cares about the humble dirtbag?

Once upon a time, in the 1950s and '60s, when countercultures were being born and postwar society was trying to get its act together, a group of young climbers set up camp in the Yosemite Valley. Out of some combination of social rebellion and love of the game, they chose to eschew jobs and traditional lifestyles in favor of scavenged food and a daily life of rock climbing and camping in the Valley for months or years at a time. They allegedly survived on cat food and thievery, and at some point, someone referred to them as a bunch of dirtbags, and the term stuck.

In all likelihood, "dirtbag" was originally intended as an insult, but as is sometimes the case with these things, the climbers, and those who followed them, took it up as a point of pride. They embraced their filthy tents and smelly-ass clothes as signs of commitment to the cause - signs that they were people willing to sacrifice for their passions, and to pursue them even as society rejected them for it.

As far as I know, there has never been a history written about the process of how the word "dirtbag" (both as a term and a lifestyle) has spread, but across the last 60 odd years, it has. And today, a quick Google search confirms that there are groups dispersed across the entire spectrum of outdoor activities that refer to themselves as dirtbags, all living a similar life of sacrificial devotion to the cause: trail runners, hikers, paddlers, skiers, climbers, world-travelers, mountain bikers, and more. Regarded as one of the best and most well-known outdoor-related podcasts of the current time, *The Dirtbag Diaries* has helped to popularize this term with its 9 million plus listeners. And a recent film backed by legendary outdoor clothing and gear company *Patagonia* that profiles the pioneering alpinist Fred Beckey was simply titled, *Dirtbag*.

The progression happened gradually, but somewhere along the way it became possible to identify dirtbags as more than just a couple of weirdos doing weirdo shit, escalating into a full-fledged counter culture embraced by thousands. In an article from her blog in 2014, ultrarunner, race director and social media influencer Candice Burt identified dirtbaggery as "a growing social movement," and she was right. The books and film adaptations of Jon Krakauer's *Into the Wild* and Cheryl Strayed's *Wild* made cult heroes out of people living dirtbag lifestyles, and a popular documentary called *Valley Uprising* was made about those original Yosemite climbers. While there's no central organizing committee, along with those popular artistic touchstones, dirtbag culture has developed its own identifiable dress code (flannels, trucker caps, cutoffs, body hair) and sacred places (Yosemite, Squamish, Patagonia, Chamonix...), and is present in beautiful outdoor locations all over the world.

Yvon Chouinard, founder of the *Patagonia* brand, and quite possibly the world's most influential dirtbag, states in his autobiography, "If you want to understand the entrepreneur, study the juvenile delinquent. The delinquent is saying with his actions, 'This sucks, I'm going to do my own thing.'"

Chouinard might not have been talking about dirtbags

specifically, but he could have been, and "This sucks, I'm going to do my own thing" summarizes the spirit of dirtbag culture as purely as anything. While the movement still might be difficult to define, there are a lot of us out there trying to figure out how to do our own thing in a world that sucks for a whole variety of reasons.

What does the dirtbag life entail?

I don't remember exactly when the concept of "dirtbagging" entered my own consciousness, but my most memorable initial encounter with the lifestyle was in getting to know Heather "Anish" Anderson, beginning at a presentation I attended where she described her experience setting a speed record during her 2013 thru-hike of the Pacific Crest Trail.

Heather was living in Washington State at the time, not far from Seattle, where my wife Angel and I had been living since 2005. We were all active members of the state's trail running community, and across time, as Angel and I got to know her, Heather's life came to exemplify, for me, what it means to live like a dirtbag.

As an athlete, Heather is a remarkable person. Like myself, she grew up as a bit of a bookish nerd in the Midwest, but she fell in love with hiking during college. Following graduation, she decided that instead of starting a career, she would thru-hike the Appalachian Trail. On that trail she adopted the trail name "Anish" - a reference to her Anishinabe heritage - and changed her entire life path. Across the last decade, she has shaped herself into one of the most notable athletes on the planet, breaking speed records on multiple American long trails that are still currently untouched by either gender.

But as a person, beyond the superhuman accomplishments, she's a total dirtbag. In order to pursue her goals, she strayed from pursuing a more traditional post-collegiate career track, choosing instead to fund summer-long hikes on the long trails through seasonal work. Heather's strategy seemed to pay off, earning her the coveted Triple Crown of long distance hiking: completing thru-hikes of the Appalachian Trail, the Pacific Crest Trail, and the Continental Divide Trail. She married another hiker and tried to settle down in Bellingham, Washington to work a straight tech job, but after just a few years, she left both her job and her marriage and dove full-on into hiking and peakbagging - setting multiple speed records across several years, and living as a full-time vagabond on occasional work and small sponsorships. At time of writing, she recently became the first woman to complete a "Calendar Year Triple Crown," spending 9 months averaging 25 miles a day to complete the more than 7000 miles of trail on the Pacific Crest Trail, Appalachian Trail, and Continental Divide Trails in a single season. That also made her the first woman to earn a "Triple Triple Crown" - completing all three long trails three times each.

If the Yosemite climbers set out the dirtbag ideal of sacrificing a normal life for the cause, Heather epitomizes it. She's placed exploration at the center of her existence, and sacrificed career, relationships, and financial stability to pursue her passions outside. And she's treated hiking, running and peakbagging as spiritual callings - not just recreational pastimes. Her whole life is defined by the pursuit of exploration and adventure, and she does it all on the cheap.

Dirtbags are everywhere

Encountering Heather's story was the first time I recognized dirtbaggery as a life strategy, but once you identify this pattern of behavior - of heeding the call of the wild, and abandoning social norms in order to immerse yourself as fully as you can in a life of exploration - you start to notice it everywhere. It manifests in different ways, but the dirtbag spirit pops-up again and again.

It's true that there are the obvious dirtbags who fit the patterns already described. In my experience within the trail running world in Washington State, I think about race directors like James Varner from *Rainshadow Running* and Candice Burt of *Destination Trail*, who got into it, in part, so they could run trail all the time and avoid working regular jobs.

But it also pops-up as a pattern among the more settled. In Tacoma, WA we know a guy named Dean Burke who's a consummate professional in his career, but spends most mornings stand-up paddleboarding on Puget Sound, encountering orcas before work, and photographing sea life that most gritty urbanite Tacomans don't even realize exists.

And as much as Dirtbag culture gets characterized as a white thing, when you travel you recognize that the same spirit is present across cultures.

In Jalcomulco, Mexico, we encountered locals who'd lived their whole lives in that small canyon town in central Veracruz, but who were managing to eke out a living as rafting or mountain biking guides, and who spent their recreational time doing the same for fun.

And in Bolivia, we encountered the phenomenon of alpinist Cholitas - traditional women, indigenous descendants of the Incas, who spend their time climbing 20,000 foot peaks in traditional garb, against social custom and popular expectation.

The dirtbag spirit manifests in different ways in different contexts, but it's a living, breathing thing.

Why are you here?

This, I suppose, brings us to the current situation, meeting here on the pages of a book about dirtbagging - me having taken the time and energy to write such a thing, and you taking the time and energy to read it.

While I can't be entirely sure what brought you here (although, let's be honest, I'm self publishing, so Hi Mom! Thanks for reading!), it's clear that some combination of factors is drawing a broad variety of people to a similar lifestyle - sacrificing the comforts of a normal life in order to play outside and explore the world.

The story that I tell myself is that some of you are here because you've gotten addicted to the feeling of "adventure" - the experience of putting yourself into situations that you aren't sure how you're going to get out of - and the personal growth that comes along with it.

And some of you are here because of the love of the game - you just really love being outside, or running, or climbing, or swimming in mountain lakes - and it feels more like a calling than a recreational pastime.

And some of you feel like life has pushed you in this direction. At some point, you developed a deep sense that something in normal life wasn't working, and that the fix was somewhere out there among the rocks and dirt and streams and oceans. You're looking for freedom, or an alternative to the pursuit of material things, or a life that is more deeply human than the one offered in the city or the suburbs.

Some of you ended up here through a long period of planning and intentional choices. Some of you maybe landed here by accident. Whatever the case, here we are, a group of dirtbags, trying to figure out what the hell we're doing with our lives.

Why am I here?

I suspect that those stories might describe you, because to some degree they all describe me.

While, when we met her, Anish became a personal dirtbag role model, the principles of a life of adventure on the cheap were things my wife and I had been learning piecemeal for years, putting together a dirtbaggy lifestyle unintentionally because we had pursued some of the same goals.

We have an unusual story by many standards. Angel and I grew up together among the cornfields in a rural area of southwestern Ohio. We started dating during high school, and married after college. Then, taking an unusual course for our peer group, we struck out to see the world. In college we took our first international trip together when Angel decided to study abroad for a semester in Australia, which we had to figure out on the cheap because we didn't have any money. While we were there, we were exposed to hordes of backpackers and vagabonds from all over the world who were traveling, and doing the same.

After that trip, we saved a couple of thousand dollars and

figured out how to move to New Zealand for 2 years. In debt, with no money, we spent a lot of our time there working, but we also bought an $800, 1986 Ford Laser and drove it around the country on weekends and holidays, scouring the South Island for beautiful spots and interesting people.

Following that trip, in a lot of ways we put our instincts towards travel and adventure on the backburner. For about 5 years after moving back to the U.S., we slogged away in the process of paying off debt and saving enough of a nest egg to be financially solvent.

But at 30, during a 1/3rd life crisis, we took up running as a means to get into shape, and discovered kindred spirits in the Seattle trail running community. We eventually progressed to running ultras, which required an increasingly unreasonable amount of time spent in the woods - most nights after work during the week, and nearly every weekend - training for these races. Trail running eventually led us back into international travel when we decided to run the Camino de Santiago in Spain. That experience facilitated a decision to quit our jobs to hike the Pacific Crest Trail. The PCT was a full immersion in dirtbag culture, as the 2650 mile trail is populated entirely by people who've quit their lives to hike and sleep outside for a summer, and most of them are doing it on the cheap.

Thru-hiking has a beautiful way of ruining people, and following the PCT we worked a couple of short-term contracts, then spent four months travelling in Latin America and two months on the road in the American West before re-establishing a base for a semi-nomadic lifestyle in the Pacific Northwest, where we started a business in the same spirit that we'd been living for several years - on the cheap, focused on adventure, and defined by travel and the outdoors.

What is this book, then?

I believe that the world changes, in both large ways and small, when people do cool things and then tell other people about how and why they did them. This book is me trying to do that. I'm trying to encapsulate how and why we've done the things we've done, as well as the how's and why's of other people we've encountered along the way.

For my part, I think the most important thing that I have to contribute to the conversation has to do with how and why it's possible to live a life full of travel and adventure as a normal person on a modest budget. And the initial idea for this book arose in that context - on a bus in Mexico in the middle of a month long trip that cost Angel and I about $1200, during a conversation about how, growing up, we never would have thought doing what we were doing was possible. Angel proposed that we should write something like a "normal person's guide to the good life," and we jotted down some initial notes in a dusty journal on that pivotal ride.

When I started actually working on this project almost a year later, I pictured it as a 20 page pamphlet - a glorified blog post - with some practical tips, mostly focused on how to save money, and focused on people like us, who wanted to figure out how to take time off to travel and explore without spending a lot of money.

This finished product is still mostly practical, and what you'll find here is, among other things, a "how to" guide about living an adventurous life on the cheap.

But the book also developed into something bigger when I

started to absorb the larger story above - that "dirtbagging" is more than just a thing people do for fun for a summer, and is actually part of a larger countercultural movement that is still relatively unformed, but has some intriguing and identifiable characteristics.

And in that spirit this book has developed, roughly, into an attempt to answer the question of what exactly it is that dirtbags are saying "sucks," and what exactly "doing our own thing" means in response.

The book is divided into five chapters, focused on major areas of life where dirtbags are charting a different path. Each will include a "Golden Rule" that states the heart of the dirtbag ethos in relation to that topic, and a discussion about concrete advice on how to live that out - from personal experience, from the experience of people cooler than myself, and from the beststuff I could find on the Googler.

In the first chapter on **Money**, we'll talk about the way that dirtbagging counteracts a prevailing story that adventure and exploration are activities accessible only to the rich and privileged, and discuss strategies for managing money that make it possible to do what you want on the cheap.

In the second chapter on **Career** we'll address the notion that your career should define you and occupy most of your time by arguing that career is a means to an end, and that adventure is an acceptable - nay, crucial - vocation. And we'll talk about the variety of strategies that people have used in the real world in order to center their lives around outdoor exploration rather than a traditional career.

When we consider **Responsibilities** I'll argue that it sucks that people think that a life characterized by dirtbagging around is irresponsible, and that those people are defining "responsibility" incorrectly. We'll talk concretely about what it actually means to be both responsible, and a dirtbag, and dive into the idea that exploration itself *is* our responsibility.

In a chapter on **Relationships**, we'll reframe the notion that relationships are a barrier to living your dirtbag dreams by pointing out that they are actually the most important avenue towards living an adventurous life. While I'm no Dear Sugar, we'll talk about some concrete advice on how to manage relationships while also living the weird-ass life of a dirtbag.

And in our final chapter on **Finding Meaning**, we'll counteract the story that's told, even by dirtbags themselves, that what we're describing here is a meaningless existence, and talk about ways that centering exploration outside can and should be an avenue towards a deeply meaningful life.

*Everything Angel and I are doing with our business is focused on living this dirtbag dream. We're called **Boldly Went** and I hope you'll check us out at **boldlywentadventures.com**, listen to the podcast (just search "Boldly Went" on any podcast app), or even better, meet us at one of our live events where we record your stories to share with the world. And if you like the book, I hope you'll sign up for our mailing list so that you can stay connected to a steady flow of inspiring stories, practical advice, and other resources for people like us, who want to actually live the lives that we daydream about. A huge amount of the material in this book has been gathered from the people whose stories are told at our events and on the podcast, so they make for a perfect way to continue the stoke beyond your reading experience here.*

CHAPTER 1: MONEY

You'd be forgiven for thinking that the trappings of the adventurous life (extended travel, taking months off from work to thru-hike, #vanlife, climbing 300 days a year) is for rich people. Indeed, all of that stuff costs money. Instagrammable Sprinters cost $70k, and American vacations can cost up to $10k a week. Most of us can't afford that shit. At the heart of the standard narrative on travel, is the notion that travel is based upon vacations, luxury, and expenses. And embedded in this claim is the idea that it is something to be indulged upon infrequently, unless of course, you are one of those rare individuals with a hearty trust fund, or other such means to travel the world at your whimsy.

The dirtbag gospel tells a different tale. At the heart of our narrative is the pronouncement that you don't have to start rich, that adventure is for everyone, and that it should be pursued as a lifestyle - not just for a week a year. If you're skeptical, the evidence is there - a long tradition of hobos, vagabonds, hikers, climbers, ski bums, and weird dudes in tropical shirts on Central American beaches has proven it.

We're starting on the topic of money, because it is the most practical thing we could discuss. It's where the rubber hits the road, and it's the little paper resource that makes everything else we'll be talking about possible. It's an eternal puzzle to be solved for the vast majority of us, but it's also a topic that dirtbag culture has a lot to say about. And the dirtbag assertion that living your dreams isn't just for rich people is, in my opinion, a life-altering contribution to the world.

But figuring out how to get there isn't automatic. It would be great if you could just decide that you're going to do whatever you want and not worry about money. It would be wonderful to float away on the winds of your whimsies, thinking everything would magically work out for you. The reality is, that's not how the world works.

Dealing with money when you don't have much of it requires some savvy strategizing, and that's what this chapter is about. It's about the financial wisdom that people living the dirtbag lifestyle have happened upon. It is that which allows them to do cool shit on the cheap, again and again, without ending up in financial ruin or massive debt.

The Golden Rule: Go as far as you can with as little as you can.

Before we dive in to practicalities, it's worth noting that money is also an appropriate place to start because our attitude towards it is maybe the most definitive aspect of the dirtbag spirit. Being a dirtbag *is* figuring out how to live your f—ing dreams even though you can't afford it. Most of us initially come to this approach to life out of necessity (because playing outside doesn't generally pay), but it's developed into a culturally defining moral principle - an ethos if you will. To be a dirtbag means to go as far as we can with as little as we can. While dirtbag culture might have started with "I guess I'll eat cat food because I bought all of that gear and only have $0.49 left to my name," it's developed into "Hell yeah I'll eat cat food, because I get it man! I don't need your fancy "people food" bullshit to be happy!"

This attitude towards money is also one of the most visible features of dirtbag culture. Dirtbags often wear their frugality as a public badge of honor. Step into any trail town during peak thru-hiker season and you'll see what I mean. It's not uncommon to see a group of dirtbag hikers strutting around town with garbage bags or rain skirts fashioned as clothing substitutes while their one and only pair of shorts and shirt go for a ride in the machines of the local laundromat. Could they go to a clothing store and buy some garb more "appropriate" for this brief pitstop in civilization? Sure. But that would cost money. And just as importantly, trying to fit in with the masses is something those dirtbags abandoned long ago.

This kind of attitude towards money isn't universal in the gear-obsessed outdoor culture, where companies like REI and Cabela's sell millions of dollars in fancy equipment each year. But dirtbags are the monks and nuns of this culture. They're the moral leaders rejecting the pursuit of wealth, choosing instead to embody the notion that there are more important things in life than material things. They assert through their actions and lifestyle that the "good life" should not be reserved for the rich. Sorry REI, but dirtbags are working to outsmart the capitalist bastards.

The Dirtbag's Financial Plan

Commitment to frugality as a moral principle has made the dirtbag community a sort of centrifuge spinning out a disproportionate amount of financial wisdom about how to be cheap in the most enjoyable ways. It has made the community a great resource for anyone trying to figure out how to make saving money less painful. If you're looking to invest more time in the things you most care about, while worrying less about how to make enough to get by, the dirtbag's financial plan is for you.

And the good news is that the financial strategies that pop up again and again - even if they take some work - aren't rocket science. They're accessible to everyone, and applicable in a variety of situations.

To illustrate why I'm confident that this is true, I'll start our discussion here by telling you a bit about my own dirtbag origin story - how my wife Angel and I learned early in our adult lives that vast realms of adventure were accessible despite the fact that we grew up as working class kids in small town Ohio.

Then, we'll identify the 9 most important financial rules that will help you to live the dirtbag dream - to go as far as you can with as little as you can, and to do amazing shit even if you don't have much money. This isn't gimmicky self-help. It's concrete wisdom congealed from a rich variety of real-life experiences from dirtbags around the world whose accomplishments serve as proof that anything is possible if you're willing to work for it.

We'll conclude this chapter with an appendix on going full dirtbag. It's chock full of the best resources I know for extending your adventure as far as you can, with as little money as possible.

Case Study: A couple of working class country kids travel the world

I, of all people, understand feeling skeptical about the idea that it's possible to escape a life defined by financial worry in order to wander off into the mountains. I was raised a few miles from the same small town in southern Ohio about which J.D. Vance wrote the book *Hillbilly Elegy*. It's the heart of the Rust Belt, and a working class place without many working class jobs. My expectation growing up was that my life would be spent living by the skin of my financial teeth. I figured that I would work full time into my 60s or 70s, and that I'd die without savings in the bank. That wasn't exactly because of personal pessimism, it was just the most common story in my town.

I was shaken out of this attitude by a girl with bigger dreams and a bigger sense of possibility. Angel and I grew up together, and started dating just before high school graduation. We maintained a long distance relationship when we attended different colleges (both in Kentucky), and during that period apart she made an audacious decision that changed our lives forever. She announced during our sophomore year that she was going to do a semester exchange in Australia.

While for some, a semester exchange might not seem like a big deal, for me, this plan sounded like a complete pipe dream. She had literally no money, and was spending all of her time and resources to pay her own way through nursing school. Neither I, nor either of our families, had anything significant to contribute towards such a trip, and to me it seemed irresponsible to even attempt such a thing.

Angel's attitude was different. She insisted that she was going to figure it out. She signed up for the program, and started hustling. Then, a couple of months later, despite my objections, she found a ticket for me on a discount airfare website and bought it with her own money. The plan was that I would come meet up with her once her study-abroad program was complete, then we would spend a month traveling around the country.

She surprised me with the ticket on Christmas morning. While I was in tears because of the level of sacrifice I knew the purchase involved, it also scared the crap out of me knowing that we literally had no money, and now had to figure out an international trip in just a couple of months. She'd spent all of her cash on flights, and I'd spent all of mine on an engagement ring (which I surprised her with on the same day - but that's a different story).

For the short version of what happened from there, despite my reservations, we figured it out. We spent our winter break scraping together as much money as we could. I worked a temp job in a factory pouring giant bags of some kind of polymer powder into a steaming vat for Toyota, and Angel picked up as many shifts as she could, wiping butts and changing bedpans as a nursing assistant.

In February, Angel flew to Perth and survived for a semester on financial aid and a small amount of savings. Along the way, she talked her way into a clinical placement with the Royal Flying Doctor Service, enabling her to travel the West Coast and fly to remote Aboriginal communities in the Outback for a couple of months on the financial backing of her program.

When I arrived in June, after her semester finished, we had about two thousand dollars in the bank. With that, we managed to bus up the East Coast, where we visited wineries, saw Steve Irwin in person, hiked around a giant island made of sand, sailed in the Whitsunday Islands, and spotted crocodiles in Cairns. We found a cheap flight that allowed us to check out Uluru, and we hung out in Perth, Adelaide, Melbourne, Brisbane, and Sydney. The trip allowed us to meet people from all around the world, and gave us experiences that changed our direction in life in massive ways. Although we came home without any money, we also achieved this adventure without having dug ourselves into a massive pile of debt.

As our first major international immersion experience, and our first big adventure together, just being in Australia was amazing for a couple of starry eyed country kids. But maybe the most transformative part of the experience came from meeting other travelers who were doing the same thing, and for much longer periods of time. As we stayed in hostels and camps along our journey, we met hundreds of backpackers from around the world - Israel, Argentina, the U.K., France, Germany, the Netherlands, Korea, Japan - who were traveling for months or years at a time on a shoestring budget. They were people like us, who were doing things that we had never realized were possible - riding scooters around Southeast Asia, packing into cramped overnight trains across China, sleeping in the dirt in the Australian Outback, trekking for weeks on end in the Himalayas - all without spending much money.

We learned, in many ways, that a lot more is possible in life than one might initially assume. We experienced it ourselves, and we met hundreds of other people along the way who were doing the same.

9 Rules to Finance your Dirtbag Dreams

I'm not telling you this story because I want the whole world to know that I saw the Crocodile Hunter in real life before he died. Although I do. He was driving a backhoe at his zoo. He was a beautiful man. God rest his soul.

Also, I'm not telling you this story because I want to present Angel and I as some kind of travel geniuses. Quite the opposite.

I'm telling you this story because it demonstrates that even a couple of average country rubes with no life experience can figure out some really cool adventures. If we can do it, you can too.

Furthermore, I'm telling you the story because it's illustrative of every other principle we'll talk about in this chapter. Our experience in Australia (I've realized in retrospect), was made possible by what I've come to think of as a dirtbag financial system. I'm not sure that I had even heard the term dirtbag used in reference to outdoor culture at the time we were on that trip, but in the years since, among dirtbag climbers, thru-hikers, ski bums, and trail runners, I've come to recognize that there are consistent financial themes that develop organically among people trying to live their dreams on the cheap. Looking back, I realize that Angel and I saw all of these at play during our first real dirtbag experience in the land Down Under.

So, without further ado, let's dive into the practical stuff, and talk about what those themes are. I'm calling them "rules," and I'll point back to our Australia trip as a concrete reference for how they work throughout our discussion. I'll also point out ways that I've seen them put into practice among other dirtbags, to give you as many ideas as I can about how you might apply the rules in your own situation to squeeze more adventure out of whatever financial resources you have available.

The "rules" are listed in no particular order, but taken as a whole they represent a comprehensive philosophy for dealing with money in a way that will maximize your ability to do cool shit, even if you're starting without much cash. All of these rules will help you overcome some of the most common financial obstacles that prevent people from taking on travel and adventure in the short term, and when followed in the long term, will help you develop a life that is defined by exploration and adventure. If you practice them diligently, you too can become a total dirtbag.

Rule 1: Scrap to Save Money

In popular imagination, dirtbags have a reputation as people who don't want to work. While it's understandable (since our preferred activities don't include traditional modes of employment), that reputation is undeserved. In lived experience, dirtbags are people who scrap constantly for money. That means both making as much money from our work as possible, and spending as little as we can to squeeze out the maximum amount from our resources.

The reasons are pretty simple: when you want to spend the majority of your time on things that don't pay you, you have to figure out how to save funds efficiently and conserve money once you have it.

Our college trip to Australia taught Angel and I that lesson early in our adult lives. Once Angel decided that we were going, the months leading up to the trip were some of the busiest of our lives. We were both full-time students, but in order to fund the trip we also had to figure out multiple ways to scrounge together cash. Angel had a marketable skill, so she worked as many hours as possible as a nursing assistant: backbreaking work that left her covered in other people's bodily fluids in exchange for $9 an hour. I was a grunt at the time, so I picked up a job in our school cafeteria, working as the university trash boy, crushing boxes and hauling food scraps in a disgusting freight elevator. Each of us realized we could make more per hour donating plasma than we could at our jobs, so we both began to religiously sell our cells to science at every chance we had.

Along with working extra, we skimped on the essentials, like food and dignity. A big part of the reason that I took up the cafeteria work rather than other options, is that I was able to eat for free while I was there, which meant only having to pay for one meal a day on average. At one point, Angel was so low on food that she made several meals from a box of Quaker oats that was infested with mealworms.

The pattern of scrapping constantly for money in any way possible is observable among dirtbags around the world. In my own experience, some of the most inspiring examples have come from Latin Americans whose national economies required them to hustle just to survive, let alone finance amazing adventures.

While traveling in Mexico a few years back, we signed up for a hiking tour in a town called Jalcomulco, near Xalapa in Veracruz State. Our guides were a couple named Karla and Antonio Rodriguez, who we became friends with over time.

They took us to their house, where they'd constructed an off-grid cabin from cinder blocks, planted their own crops, and raised chickens and honey bees. Living there, they could survive on about $50 U.S. per month, producing almost zero waste. Lest you project images of developing nation poverty onto them, they were both university trained and qualified professionals. Karla has a law degree and Antonio studied biology. Antonio travels around the world working as a kayak guide, they run several side hustle businesses, and they aren't desperate for cash in any serious way. They're just dirtbags, and they've meticulously organized their life in order to spend very little money.

While we were in Bolivia, I took some English lessons from a local guy in Sucre named Vini Paniagua who we've also gotten to know well. Bolivia is the poorest country in South America, but despite working as a normal guy in a tough economy, in the two years since we met him he's managed to figure out how to travel all over the U.S. and South America. To get there, he's worked as a semi-professional soccer player, a veterinarian, an English Teacher, a volunteer coordinator, and a counselor at a camp for children with developmental disabilities. He is also learning to brew beer. He's a quintessential hustler who's figured out how to maximize the resources he has in order to live a remarkable life.

Closer to home, through an event we organized with Boldly Went in Portland, Oregon, we got to know Gracetopher Kirk (who is gender non-binary, and prefers "they/them" pronouns). When we met them they were recovering from a broken back and a resulting extended period off of work, but they were planning to hike the Pacific Crest Trail in a couple of months anyway. In the interim, they set up a Patreon account where sponsors could give money in exchange for poetry and updates along the trail, and gathered hiking supplies for free or cheap. They made their tent from tarp and strings they found in the trash, and although injury knocked them off of the trail midway through, they still managed a thousand mile hike on next to no money in 2018. Now, they're busy hustling in a restaurant job saving up for a move to Germany. No money, no prospects, just a lot of vision and belief in their ability to figure it out.

Far from being averse to work, the thing that unites all of those people is that they are scrappers. They make money in a variety of ways, and avoid spending it as much as they can. And that approach has allowed all of them to do remarkable things on limited resources for extended periods of time.

Rule 2: Start with what you have, rather than what things "cost".

If you want to get comfortable with taking on big, crazy challenges, it's important to think in terms of possibilities rather than limitations. To make it concrete in our current context, when you're thinking about funding a life of adventure, it's important to start with how much money you actually have, rather than starting by thinking about how much what you want potentially costs.

This isn't just a motivational speech about changing your attitude - although attitude is part of it. It's a concrete strategy on how to make decisions about how you'll spend your money. I've found that a great way to be sure that you spend your money most efficiently is to consider how you can get the most out of what you have, rather than deciding you want something, seeing how much it costs, and saving up for it. The reason being, is that in actuality, "cost" is frequently not a fixed unit for things like travel and adventure. You can almost always get what you want for less than the first price that pops up on an internet search.

Once again, we learned this lesson concretely on our Australia trip. When we were planning our month of travel, my initial internet search for potential options killed my enthusiasm. Every tour, hotel, and flight seemed to carry a price tag that would break our budget. So, I resigned myself to the idea that Angel and I might just spend a month hanging around Perth where she was finishing her exchange program. That wouldn't be that bad.

But when I actually arrived on the ground in Australia, we sat down with the couple thousand U.S. dollars we had saved, and got practical. With a little bit of research, we found cheap plane tickets to Adelaide on the East Coast, and started thinking about possibilities. We asked around to some of the friends Angel had made, and realized we could save on accommodation and food by staying with people they knew in several cities along the way. Then, because of the distances we were travelling, we realized we could further save on accommodation by booking overnight buses. The minor discomfort of sleeping on a bus, rather than a motel, could afford us more money to spend doing cool stuff. We decided to go for it, bought the tickets, and figured it out. Instead of hanging out in Perth for a month, we spent three weeks of our trip exploring the East Coast from Adelaide in the far south, to Cairns in the far north.

A principle that was at play on that trip, is that you can get to the same goal using vastly different financial strategies, and if you have to, you can probably figure out how to do what you want for less.

When we hiked the Pacific Crest Trail years later, it was a great place to observe this principle in action. A long trail is essentially a blank canvas. On the PCT, you start in Mexico with one goal: of making it to Canada. How do you do that? By figuring shit out using whatever resources you have.

We hiked the trail in 2015. From the beginning, it was clear that the ways and means of completing the journey were as varied as the 1500 plus people out there hiking. One guy we heard about, but didn't meet, hired someone to drive his RV between trailheads for the summer so he could crash and refuel as comfortably as possible every time the trail crossed a road. The amount he was spending to hike could have likely funded a dozen hikers who were going in pure dirtbag style. Our friend, whose trail name was "The Jesus," employed a strategy of stark contrast; he used only the gear he already owned before the trail, spent a lot of his rest days in the woods rather than in town, and rarely seemed to stop in restaurants or hotels. Both strategies got the hikers from Mexico to Canada. The amount of money they spent was exponentially different however.

The dirtbag wisdom in all of this, is that your resources can be stretched as far as you want them to be when it comes to travel and adventure. Wilderness or bandit camping, dumpster diving, walking, biking, and hitchhiking are free anywhere in the world. Costs go up from there depending on your preferences. So the best approach is to think about how you can use what you have to get as far as you want, rather than getting bogged down in what such things purportedly "cost".

Rule 3: Go where you can afford.

Whether domestic or abroad, a fundamental principle of dirtbag culture is to save money and stretch your resources further by picking your location carefully. It's a basic lesson: where you are determines what you get.

This principle is perhaps most nakedly apparent during international travel experiences, and it's one that dirtbags have been taking advantage of for generations - at least since California beach bums discovered the surf breaks on the Baja Peninsula.

On a four month trip around Latin America a few years ago, Angel and I came into contact with a slew of people who were living out dreams that they wouldn't have been able to afford in their home countries, simply because they realized their money would stretch further abroad. We started our trip in Guatemala, because it's perhaps the world's best place to learn a bit of Spanish on a budget (20 hours of one-on-one lessons a week, plus accomodations and three meals a day cost Angel and I $200 per person in 2016). At our school, we met a woman named Elizabeth who was experiencing burnout from waitressing work. She wanted to take several months off, so she decided to maximize her time by going somewhere cheaper than the United States. We lost track of her after we finished at the school, but thanks to the magic of social media, a few months later we ran into each other again in Patagonia, after she'd bussed, and then hitched, the 5000 mile length of South America. She was purchasing tickets home because she'd finally run out of money, but on a budget that would have been blown in a couple of weeks in the U.S., she had managed to spend months enjoying an epic adventure through Latin America.

In the same region, we met Mexican vagabonds who'd traveled Central America on motorcycles, Floridian early retirees living luxuriously in Costa Rica, and young Texans who fell into the vortex of surfing and surviving on hospitality work in San Juan del Sur, Nicaragua. All of them were having massive life experiences that were made possible primarily because of where they chose to do them.

I'm a proponent of taking your travel dollars to the places they are most needed, so I say go where places are cheap and the economy is weak. Not only is it a lot of fun, but you'll be helping support people who could really use it.

The principle of stretching your money further by choosing your location wisely doesn't just apply in the developing world however. When traveling internationally in more expensive countries, choosing to hang out in places with favorable exchange rates can be a game changer. A major reason that we were able to do so much more than I'd expected with our money in Australia was that we were there, by happy accident, at a time when the U.S. dollar was extremely strong against the Australia dollar, so as soon as our plane landed, we essentially doubled our money. The $2000 or so dollars we'd saved at home, as if by magic, became $4000.

If you're reading from virtually any English speaking country, you can be assured that there are places all over the world where dollars and pounds will stretch much further than at home. It would be hard (though not impossible for the dirtbaggiest of you) to spend a month in Australia for U.S. $1000/person these days. However, it's still possible in places like Spain, Chile, Portugal, and Croatia - not to mention most of Latin America, Southeast Asia, and Eastern Europe. Global exchange rates are in constant flux, so just do some Google research beforehand.

And even if you're traveling domestically, every country has places that are more expensive than others. To use the U.S. as an example, a road trip through California can cost significantly more than through New Mexico or Montana. And a week in Sedona could cost you three times as much as you'd pay for the same scenery and outdoor experience in a weird little town in Utah. Every expensive country I'm aware of has rad, off the beaten path options that are significantly cheaper than the most popular tourist destinations. Doing a little research and finding the less expensive spots can mean more fun for a lot less money.

And like every "rule" we're discussing here, the principle of going where you can afford is a great strategy for life - not just for travel. It is applicable with common sense decisions at a micro level. For instance, don't go to expensive restaurants or hotels, because you can get a bed and food for much less. Feeling thirsty? Grab a couple beverages from the bodega instead of the bar. On the move? Use public transit in place of Uber. And even if you have some higher ticket items on the "must do" list, ask around or look online for coupons, discount codes, and other deals. You'd be surprised how many bargains are out there if you're willing to do even a small amount of work to look for them.

I would also encourage you to consider this principle when you're thinking about major life decisions, like where to live, where to study, where to work, and when and where to retire. If you are willing to explore a bit, you'll find that your options in life are dramatically broader than if you lock yourself in to one locale. Major adventures that might seem like impossibilities at home can be realistic if you travel. Whether it's starting your own business, becoming a digital nomad, taking months or years off from work to hike or climb, or even to retire early, your options expand when you research other locations.

Rule 4: Cut out the things you don't care about

If we define "simplicity" as getting rid of the crap that you don't need, then virtually every classic dirtbag endeavor lends itself to simple living - from van life, to the Great Western Road Trip, to thru-hiking, to ski bumming, to busing around Patagonia, to living in a tent in the Yosemite Valley. If you're living out of a car, backpack, or tent, life is just easier if you only carry the essentials. It's no surprise then, that this type of simplicity has become a core commitment of dirtbag counter culture.

We'll talk more later about why the dirtbag's commitment to the simple life is important for a variety of reasons, but for now it's worth noting that this type of cutting the fat is a solid financial principle.

While "you should buy less" is self-evidently good advice if you're trying to save money, it can also be hard advice to take. Most of us don't *want* to buy less, because it sounds like sacrifice. After all, we typically buy things because we *want* them, so buying less means having less of the things that we want.

A solid piece of dirtbag wisdom is that this doesn't always have to be the case. When you're forced to skimp, you learn that there are a lot of things that can be cut out of your budget with little to no negative effect on your quality of life. Most people, whether they realize it or not, buy a bunch of shit that they *don't* need or want.

As a short-term travel principle, we learned this as an easy fix because of our limited resources in Australia. We didn't have enough for the full complement of travel offerings, so we did our best to cut out everything we didn't care about. For instance, we spent zero dollars on alcohol and cooked the vast majority of our own meals. We didn't go to many shows or tours; instead we spent most of our sightseeing time wandering around on foot or on public transit. We saved a ton of money on accomodations by staying in hostels, utilizing backpacking campgrounds, and sleeping on overnight buses on the way to our next destination. We didn't really drink at the time, and we didn't care about fancy hotels or nice restaurants because we were after an epic travel experience, so none of that felt like a sacrifice. No harm, no foul.

As a life principle, this is one of the most fulfilling pieces of dirtbag financial advice to apply comprehensively. You just *feel* better when you don't waste money on things that don't actually improve your life. This doesn't have to imply a radical lifestyle change. If you just avoid buying new clothes or cars or houses or furniture when yours still work, it's enough to make a difference for most people. You might feel cheap at first if you keep old crap around until it's broken or torn, but pretty soon you'll start to feel like you're outsmarting the people around you that are dumping money into frivolities. You'll meet other people who share your ethos, so the social pressures will dissipate, and you'll start to notice a difference in your budget. When you use the money you save on something you actually *do* care about, you'll feel like the secret to a happy life is to become a frugal-ass bastard.

Unlike some types of discipline, in my experience, this type of frugality is actually addictive, because it's invigorating to practice. This, I think, is the reason that a lot of people who dive into the dirtbag lifestyle find themselves ruined for a normal life. Our friends Matt and Julie Urbanski, who we'll talk about again in the next chapter on career, thru-hiked early in their 20s, and during the years after have never really recovered. They have frequently cited it as their ideal goal to survive only with what they can carry on their backs, and for a decade they've lived not far off of that goal, living on the road or in apartments that they rent fully furnished, storing the few things they do own in their family homes in Ohio.

And after spending their early lives as working stiffs, Ras and Kathy Vaughan have spent the bulk of the last few decades traveling through life light and fast, owning little and experiencing a lot. They have worked as house sitters to survive by essentially borrowing housing and furniture. They have grown much of their own food, and have been ski resort employees to engage in a favorite activity without cost during the winter. A few years back, they took on the name "Team UltraPedestrian" and started using the freedom they'd cultivated to develop crazy long distance projects, both on trail and on the snow. Through these projects they successfully obtained sponsorship to avoid paying for a lot of their gear. Among other things, Ras completed a six time crossing of the Grand Canyon, and as a couple they designed and completed a 2600 mile thru-hiking loop through Oregon, Washington and Idaho. They own just a little, but they experience a hell of a lot.

It might sound simplistic, but it's true: most people buy a lot of things that either don't improve their lives, or even limit them. If you cut those things out, you'll be left with resources to invest in things that you actually do care about.

Rule 5: If you can get the same thing for less, do it.

The best plan to save money is to not buy anything. But if you can't do that, a related trick of the dirtbag trade is to figure out ways to get the same things for less. Taking this approach on as a life commitment will make you seem like a Depression-era grandpa, but hey, who knows better how to stretch a penny?

Budget airlines, public transit rather than rental cars, groceries rather than restaurants, walking rather than taxis, hostels or couchsurfing rather than hotels, self-guided rather than guided tours - all of those things have been staples of existence for Angel and I since our trip to Australia, because they were essential to our existence while we were there. For extending short-term travel when you're on a budget, the cheapest option is almost always the best option.

But living like a penny-pinching grandpa is also a powerful formula for financial success in the long term. This calculation is a little bit crude, but the principle is true enough: if you can figure out how to save 10% on your regular expenditures, by the end of a 70 year lifespan you will have given yourself 7 years of financial freedom.

When you live for months at a time in a van without an income, you realize quickly that small things matter. Meals, groceries, gas, toiletries, electronics - all of it adds up quickly. Across a lifetime, if you purchase all of your clothes, computers, phones and furniture used or on clearance, all of your groceries at outlet prices, and all of your gas at the cheapest pump in town, the savings will add up to 5 - 6 figures against standard prices for new products.

It's also solid advice to look for durable brands with lifetime warranties - keep your eyes open at the thrift store, or even buy them new if you can afford to pay the higher upfront cost. They aren't the only ones with this policy, but I'm loyal to the brand *Patagonia* entirely because of their warranty. When their products tear, break or wear out, they keep their word to repair, recycle, or replace them, no matter how old they are, how much you've used them, or if your friend gave them to you as a hand-me-down. If you obtain one of their coats now - even at a thrift store -you theoretically will never have to pay for another coat again. It's an environmental commitment on their part, but it's a great financial benefit for the average dirtbag.

Being a cheap-ass on large purchases matters even more than day-to-day expenditures, and is a more perilous endeavor. On houses, cars, education, and the like, even small percentages in savings can equal thousands of dollars over time.

Unfortunately, as every car salesman and loan officer knows, due to some cruel trick of human psychology, the bigger the purchase we're making, the easier it is to rationalize massive additional costs. With education, for example, the difference between $12,000/year and $14,000/year for college tuition can sound almost negligible, when in reality it adds up to $8,000 in additional debt even before interest accrues on the loans you probably have to take out. That would pay for a six month trip around the world after you graduate. And with cars, the difference between $5,000 and $8,000 for a used Toyota may seem minor, but the cost equates to an entire month of work at a decently paying job. An extra $100/month in rent might not sound like much when you're signing a lease, but across 30 years it amounts to $36,000 extra dollars, or two years of comfortable living on a beach in Mexico.

Because of the commitment to get things as cheaply as possible, and because I believe in the intrinsic value of both travel and education, I'm also a big proponent of North Americans looking abroad for their higher education, if they choose to pursue one. While the cost of university in much of the English-speaking world has largely spiraled out of reasonable control, almost unbelievably for an American, there are countries where you can obtain a degree, taught in English, for free or nearly so, even if you're an international student. And they're cool places, like Norway and Germany and Malaysia. It might take a bit of upfront work and out-of-the-box thinking, but student visas tend to be relatively easy to obtain, and I can't think of a better deal than spending a couple of years abroad, studying for free, and leaving with a quality education and zero life-destroying debt.

On every purchase, big or small, the dirtbag's wisdom is to just get what you need, while getting the most affordable version of it that you can. Maximizing the amount of adventure you can fit into life requires this type of approach, and while all of this might make you seem crazy cheap, I say you'll be crazy cheap like a fox.

Rule 6: Friends make life cheaper.

A theme that will come up repeatedly in this book is that living the dirtbag dream is all about participating in the community of amazing people who are stoked about this kind of thing.

We'll talk about the kumbaya portion of this principle later. For now, let's point out that there are solid, practical financial reasons to be cool and make friends.

It's as true in travel as in life that going with another person is usually cheaper than going solo, assuming that they aren't the type of person who's going to convince you to waste your money and booze it up all of the time. When you go with a partner, you can split costs on things like food, transportation and accommodations. Having a friend or partner equals automatic savings. The fact that it's cheaper to do life together is a big reason that in much of the world, communal dwelling and packed public transit is standard. When you don't have much money, you figure out exactly what needs to be owned, what can be shared, and what can be gone without.

The "friends make life cheaper" principle extrapolates out geographically as well. If you have friends scattered around a variety of cool places, it's possible that they can not only provide you with a free place to crash, but also share with you the "local knowledge" of the area. It's like having your very own tour guide and travel advisor when you're out there on the road. Only this tour guide won't charge you exorbitant fees. Nor will they take you on some "cookie cutter" tour of the area where you'll fight your way through hordes of tourists only to walk away with a superficial experience and some strange souvenir magnet to put on your fridge.

Our Australian introduction to this idea took place in Adelaide - the first stop on our East Coast tour. A couple of contacts that Angel had made through friends in Perth were an older couple named Fran and Bronte. They hosted us, and took us on a personalized tour of the city in a 1930s era "Hupmobile," which apparently was a popular type of car at the time, and introduced us to "Pie Floaters" (a meat pie smothered in pea soup) which apparently is a type of food. We had a much richer experience of their city than if we'd paid for a hostel and done backpacker tours, and they spotted us for virtually all of it. All told in Australia, we crashed at friends' houses for about two weeks of our month of travel, and it was a huge part of the reason we were able to make the trip work.

I don't want to say that we're all a bunch of calculating freeloaders, but I do think that the money saving benefits of extensive friend networks has played a big role in the development of dirtbag culture as a largely communal one. In the thru-hiking community, you can see this pragmatism at play in the practice of "Yogi-ing," a subtle art that involves striking up conversations - usually with day hikers - in the hopes that they will offer you snacks, a ride into town, or even a couch to crash on. It's considered shameful to ask directly for these things, but if you simply behave like the type of person that a stranger would want to offer food, a beer, or a place in their home for the night in exchange for regaling them with stories of adventure and humorous anecdotes from the trail, then you've both made a new friend and you got that burger you've been thinking about for days. Everyone wins.

Even with Yogi-ing, where a filthy thru-hiker specifically angles for an innocent bystander's PBR, the ultimate goal (in the best cases anyway) is to create a relationship that's mutually beneficial. In my experience, the dirtbag community has taken shape as an extensive network of these types of relationships. Everywhere I've been, communal sharing among friends has been something I've observed directly. Whether it's our thru-hiking friend Six2 living in shared housing with vegan anarchists in Portland, our friend Danger Muffin crashing on our couch for a weekend so he doesn't have to sleep in his Subaru again, my climber friend Janet partnering with a neighbor to co-parent a cat so she can be away from home for weeks at a time, or the dirtbags in Squamish letting us set up our tent at their $10 a night camp, dirtbags share things readily. Sure, there's some pragmatism there; using other people's stuff is cheaper. But also, the expectation is that you'll pay it forward. Maintaining community is fun, and you'll waste less. So even if we're all Yogi-ing each other a bit, it's a great system to be a part of in the end.

Communal camping, hostels, and bars are classic places to start making dirtbag friends beyond the crag, trail, or gym. But the internet has also spawned some great resources that facilitate the process of getting to know people and saving money at the same time. "Warm Showers" is a questionably named network of bike touring enthusiasts who provide accommodation and support for others who are coming through their town, and "Couchsurfing.com" is the classic free way to find a spot to crash in a stranger's home - or to let a stranger crash in yours. Airbnb, of course, offers a similar experience for various levels of cost, and while you have to pay, it's also more likely that your hosts will clean up the place before you arrive.

Rule 7: Don't let going broke stop you.

When we started meeting other backpackers on our trip to Australia, it didn't take long for us to figure out that we were amateurs. Not long into our trip, we began to take note of huge numbers of internationals who were travelling not just for months, but for years at a time.

My initial assumption was that these people must be trust funders, or at least have a parent who was financing their trip, but we made a couple of friends from the U.K. named Tom and Nicola who explained the actual situation to us. Most of these travelers just knew something that we didn't in our youthful naivete. When you run out of cash, you can just find work along the way.

In Tom and Nic's case, they were out for a year on a world tour. They hadn't planned it this way, but in their enthusiasm they over spent during their time in Australia. They ran out of cash, and were forced to spend four months working in Brisbane in customer service jobs to replenish their bank accounts. Although this wasn't what they had envisioned when they first set out, they made the most of it, and this stop to work meant the difference between going home and continuing to explore. We met them in a place called Fraser Island, just after they had finished their time in Brisbane, but we know their strategy worked out for the best because we met up with them again in Chicago six months later - long after we'd returned home, they were still out exploring the world.

The inspirational message in that story is that there's no reason to get all down and defeated if you plan an epic adventure, but instead crash and burn and go broke in Brisbane. You can always pick yourself up, get a job, and keep going.

The practical message is that, if you want to, you can stretch out a travel experience indefinitely by getting jobs along the way.

We didn't realize that this was an option simply because we hadn't traveled abroad before, and if you haven't travelled, it's easy to assume that you can't work in most countries due to visa issues. It's easy to think that you can't just show up in a random country and expect to work whenever you want.

That's true, but only partially. Many countries offer travelers working holiday visas that will allow you to live and work for six months to a year, and even if you're in a country where this isn't the case, there are thousands of options in most countries to work on a volunteer basis. While these positions won't pay in cash, many of them will provide you with what you need - food and shelter. These types of jobs range from scrubbing toilets in a hostel, to assisting economic development organizations. The possibilities in-between are nearly infinite.

Backpackers' hostels are the classic hub for these types of jobs, and it's a tried and true strategy to just show up at one (or give them a call) and ask if they're hiring, or know anyone who is.

If you do a bit more preplanning, you'll find an increasing number of options for online freelance work that can be done from anywhere with a wifi connection. While much of this requires training, it isn't impossible to find entry-level work to get your foot in the door. Alternately, there are also relatively straightforward qualifications you can get (like teaching English for example), that will allow you to get hired for temporary positions legally and ethically all over the world. People travel for years this way.

Of course, if you're travelling in your own country, you can always just get a job when you run out of cash without stressing about things like visas and legality. For U.S. readers, in my own anecdotal experience, it seems that every restaurant and brewery in Bend, Truckee, Bishop, Telluride, Moab, and Durango is staffed entirely by dirtbags who ran out of money and decided to stay in place rather than going back home.

The important thing to remember is this: running out of cash is not the same thing as failure. It just means that you're going to have to get creative to figure out how to keep going. Keep fighting!

We'll discuss this more in the next chapter, but some of my favorite online resources for dirtbags looking for jobs and volunteer opportunities to cover costs both before and while travelling include workaway.info, hosteljobs.net, and helpx.net. They are all specifically focused on jobs for travelers and have positions listed all over the world. For more niche careers, another great option is organic farm volunteering, or "WOOFing" - a strategy so common among international travelers that it's become a verb. For dirtbags in the U.S. with time to plan ahead, it's also a great option to check out the job site for the National Park Service. And JobMonkey.com is aimed specifically at people looking for "cool jobs," and has a great directory for ski bums.

Rule 8: Kill debt and save money.

The distilled essence of the dirtbag dream life is the ability to explore and adventure however, and wherever, the wilderness calls you.

And if you state the big picture implications of that concretely, from a financial perspective, the ultimate dirtbag dream looks like complete financial freedom - the ability to *pay* for your adventures when you want to, and freedom from debt that prevents you from focusing on them.

If you're at a stage of life where that type of financial freedom seems like a ludicrous fantasy, it's worth noting that most of us actually *do* get there by the time we're in our 60s or 70s. It's called retirement. A savvy few get there earlier. And some of the lucky bastards reading this have already achieved it. The question to ask is: "how?"

While it hasn't been stated directly, all of the principles we've been talking about have, in fact, been developed with the goal of financial freedom in mind. They are all focused on bringing down the cost of life and adventure as much as possible. If you can learn to be happy with $20k per year, you will achieve financial freedom much more easily than if you are committed to a $75k per year lifestyle.

But discovering the Holy Grail of real, long-term financial freedom - that is, setting your life up so that you don't have to work for money ever again - is next-level shit. The people who achieve it before retirement age, especially the people who don't start with money, don't arrive just by lowering their cost of living. They adopt a long-term financial strategy and devote themselves to it for decades.

While I'm not going to be able to provide a comprehensive outline of that strategy here, I'd be remiss if I didn't talk, at least a bit, about how people manage to go beyond just cutting costs to that next level - of affording to do what they want all the time. And while the idea of "financial freedom" is like the Hunt for Eldorado (it's enchanting, complicated, and hundreds of books have been written about it), in broad outline, the fundamentals behind a long-term strategy to get there are relatively simple: kill your debt and squirrel away as many resources as you possibly can, starting now.

Easy, right?

I know - things are more complicated than that. But adopting a few broad strategies around debt and savings is achievable for anyone.

Generally speaking, I think the motivation to avoid debt comes naturally when you do the things that dirtbags do - like take long periods of time off of work. Debt is is a commitment that you take on now that determines what your actions will be in the future. For someone who craves freedom, it feels like a millstone, and the opposite of the goal. When you aren't working, the weight of debt on your shoulders can be soul crushing. It's natural to *want* to avoid it.

In general, I think that is a solid instinct; following it can help you avoid a lot of day-to-day financial pitfalls. Many of the most common types of debt (sourced from predatory lenders like credit card companies and payday loan providers with double-digit interest rates), can turn something as simple as a trip to the grocery store into a year of suffering. It's not incidental to all of the good memories of Australia I've been talking about that neither Angel or I had credit cards on that trip, so there was no possibility of financial hangover afterwards. High interest debt, in my opinion, is a universal evil. It will kill your soul and ruin your fun.

But even so called "good debt," like low interest rate mortgages, automobile loans, and student loans, should be approached with a healthy dose of caution. While those types of debt can be used to purchase things that are either necessary (or will be a net financial benefit in the end), they also represent a devil's wager because of the significant costs in terms of freedom. The decision to sign a mortgage typically ties you down for 30 years - the majority of your adult life - if you pay the minimum. Unless you learn a marketable, lucrative skill, student loans frequently don't actually "pay for themselves" as reliably as they used to, and payments can stretch out for decades. If you're cash poor, low cost, practical programs at community or technical colleges can make for much better financial decisions than traditional universities.

Sometimes the universe screws you over with accidents and medical bills. After all, shit happens. But when you are considering taking on debt of your own free will, here are some points to consider: a) How much will you benefit from what you're buying? b) How long will it take you to pay it off? c) How much it is going to impact your life to make your payments? Student loans may well be a good decision if they give you the earning potential to pay them off in a couple of years, and then provide for a significant amount of financial freedom afterwards. A mortgage might be a great idea if you're planning to be in one place for a long time, have the skills to fix and flip, or if you are able to rent the place out for enough to cover the costs of ownership. But if either of those loans are big enough that they'll prevent you from doing anything but working for decades at a time, even a net financial win in the end might not be enough to make it worth it if long-term adventure is your goal.

Whatever type of debt we're talking about, I'm still a firm believer in hustling to kill it as soon as possible - even if that's a decades-long process - starting first with the highest interest loans and working down from there.

The flip side of killing debt is saving up across the long term. When I was young, my family used to tell a (maybe apocryphal) story about a great uncle who everyone had assumed was poor because he lived in a shack and spent like a miser. When he died, however, it was discovered that he had left a million dollars buried in coffee cans in his backyard. Although I wish that he had been able to have a little more fun in life, he was a real inspiration. His story taught me a valuable lesson: the more you can save when you're working, the more freedom you'll have when you aren't.

Nowadays there are more sophisticated and effective ways to stash your money, and while this might not seem quintessentially dirtbaggy, I'm in favor of professionalizing that process rather than just stashing cash away in cans. Due to the rules of compound interest, the difference between dollars sitting in a hole, and an investment earning even a measly 6% interest across time, can mean many thousands of dollars depending on how much you're putting away.

I'm also in favor of automating your savings, if possible. If you're working in a long-term job, it's a good idea to have a percentage of your income removed from your paycheck and placed in an account that you can't (or won't) touch. In general, we spend what we have in our pocket, so if you can place a portion of your income somewhere safe, you'll protect it for the future.

It takes a bit more work, but planning for the long term, and dedicating yourself both to a day-to-day lifestyle of simplicity, and a big-picture savings and debt reduction plan, can help you become a next-level dirtbag with a significant amount of financial freedom. You *can* set yourself up with a significant amount of time and money to spend running off into the woods, even if you don't start with all that much.

I believe in the power of combining the rules we've talked about in this chapter with a long-term commitment to paying down debt and saving up cash because it worked for us.

A few months after returning from our trip to Australia, Angel and I graduated from college with about $70k in student loan debt. Within 2 years we racked up about $10k more. Then we bought a condo. By 25 years old, we were in debt to the tune of

$250k. All things considered, it wasn't an outrageous amount, and it was mostly "good" debt, but it was still a far cry from being debt-free. Across the following decade, we practiced everything we've been talking about here, and even living primarily on nursing salaries, we managed to get ourselves entirely out of debt, all the while burying a fair amount of money in the proverbial "backyard". Now, at 38, we just worry about paying our day-to-day expenses and putting a bit away for retirement. We haven't achieved full financial freedom, but we've gone from $250k in the hole to a decent amount of money in the bank - and we've still had pretty damn good lives along the way.

Because we started from a low baseline, I really do believe that it's possible. For some, it will mean a sustained commitment over a couple decades. But in essence, that's just a commitment to live the way we've been talking about here anyway - like a total dirtbag.

"Desk to Dirtbag" is a great online resource that is focused on helping you apply this type of system in your own situation. The author is a guy who spent years figuring out how to live fancy free on the road in his truck drifting around South America. The financial section of his blog is a great place to start because he deals with debt, investment and financial freedom extensively.

I've never read it, but I've heard a lot of people say that you should check out the classic book "Your Money or Your Life" by Vicki Robin and Joe Dominguez.

If you're interested in more personalized financial advice, you could always pay a financial advisor. But there are also plenty of free ways to learn what you need to know and develop a long-

term financial plan. Nerdwallet.com is a good resource you can access online, for instance.

Rule 9: If you can, leave for that big adventure right now.

The concluding rule in this chapter is also the simplest, and probably the most important:

If you can, leave for that adventure right now.

While I think you can learn a lot from books like this one, as a coworker once said, "Sometimes life don't take thinkin', it takes doin'."

After he said that, he attempted to climb a ladder that wasn't properly secured. It collapsed under his body weight, and he went tumbling to the concrete floor. He was out of work for a week. Still, I think this story is appropriate because it illustrates my larger point: sometimes you can only learn the lessons you need to learn if you do the things you want to do.

All of the rules we've talked about in this chapter are disciplines to be practiced, and the only real way to learn how they will play themselves out in your life is to begin actually practicing them. Since a grand adventure, tackled on a shoestring, is such a great immersion experience in the fundamentals of dirtbaggery, there's nothing more financially valuable that you can do for yourself. Or at least nothing more financially valuable that is also as fun!

It's not that important what the actual adventure is. Follow your heart. Take a month off and drive around in your car running trails as you find them. Hang out in Red Rock and climb all winter. Bus around Mexico. Fly to Spain and walk the

Camino. It doesn't really matter, as long as you find a way to get rid of everything inessential and live on as little as you can, for as long as you can, exploring. Let yourself be formed by the experience and see what happens.

It's a huge advantage if you decide to go for it while you're young. Angel and I were lucky to have landed in Australia when we were 21, while we were still forming our life patterns. It has shaped our whole approach to finances, work, and life in general, and that's put us in a great spot now that we've hit middle age. The trip got us hooked on adventure, and it also got us stashing away funds in a way that's been a huge benefit as we've gotten older.

If you're in your teens or 20s, it's important to know that the sooner you can build smart habits with your money, the longer you will have to capitalize on your savings. This is true not only in the most obvious sense (money saved can grow as it accrues interest over time), but also in the fact that your skill with managing money - your financial discipline, discretion, decision making, resourcefulness - will also grow as you practice and refine your strategies year after year.

But grand adventure has its value at every stage of life. If you're mid-career, you likely have a lot more financial stability than the youngsters do, so you are likely risking less by running off into the woods. You're probably less replaceable at work, and they'll be more likely to negotiate a bit of leave. It will also feel really liberating to take that time away after all of this time spent working, and you'll be able to take pride in doing something productive with your midlife crisis rather than having an affair or buying a convertible. You'll feel fit and alive in ways you perhaps haven't experienced in years, and you'll knock yourself out of any rut that you might find yourself in. Take your partner and kids if you have them. They're going to love it too.

And if you've made it to your Golden Years, you may realize that you're already where most of us dream of being. If you've put some money back, learning to be happy on a dirtbag's budget may show you that your options for early retirement to a life of adventure are wide open. You may find that a little exploration is what you needed to kick-off your next stage in life, and may provide the motivation to keep moving into old age.

Why wait? Go now.

Conclusion

To conclude this chapter, rather than rehashing what has already been said, I want to step back and paint a picture of the life that can be made possible by following all of the "rules" we've been discussing. While we've talked about a series of separate ideas, I believe the whole is greater than the sum of the parts. That whole, is the lifestyle payoff that ultimately makes all of these rules worth following.

I would claim that the lifestyle that is possible by following the strategies listed above, represents an alternative reality to the one you'll arrive at by following a standard life path. It is a deviation from the "white picket fence" scenario that has long been at the heart of the socially conditioned perspective on life and success, at least here in the United States. This typical perspective on success is based upon amassing material goods and comforts, watching cable television on the newest flat-screen television set, paying for expensive dinners out at the "nice" restaurants, stuffing our closests to the brim with the latest fashions and trends - all of this while incurring massive amounts of debts that leave us silently imprisoned in a life that we may not have actually been consciously creating in the first place. To me (and to those who desire a life beyond the drudgery of this work-a-day existence), the words of Henry David Thoreau capture this sentiment with poignance and clarity: "Most men lead lives of quiet desperation and go to the grave with the song still in them." It is this song - the impulse to do more, the drive to seize the day, the longing for a life of greater fulfillment - that the dirtbag ethos is so ardently fueled by. It is the recognition that there is a better way; that, despite what you may have been told, it's ok to "color outside the lines." In fact, it's *the* way. The financial principles contained in this chapter present a way out of a life of desperation. They present a way to achieve the dream life of travel, adventure, excitement, and spontaneity. They offer us a way to transcend the status quo in favor of creating a life that is infinitely more enjoyable. In short, they empower us to find our voice; for in the end, it is the song that really matters.

Now, I don't want to paint an over-glorified picture here. Yes, this life is possible. Throughout this book, I will share multiple stories of people out there in the world proving that this is so. However, like most things that are *actually* worth having, it will take some work. It will also take some sacrifice. On the surface it'll be less shiny. Your furniture, phones and computers will be bought used or three generations behind. People may not be impressed by your old, beat-up car or your simple, modest house (if you even have those things). Your thrift store wardrobe may lend to a quasi-hobo-like appearance, prompting your friends to question your life decisions.

In a lot of ways it won't be easy. You'll spend a lot of time scrapping for cash, likely working more than one job or developing side hustles that you can do on the weekend. If you study, you may go to a less expensive community college that no one is impressed by. When you go to work, there's a good chance you'll be chomping on a pb&j while you watch your co-workers indulge in expensive takeout. There may be times when you won't experience the immediate social benefits of your hard work like they do. You'll feel jealous when you see their new cars and fancy houses. You may catch your ego asking questions like "What the hell are you doing?" There may even be times where the social pressure gets so strong that it feels like a rip tide trying to draw you back into the comfort and false security of conformity.

But all of that hard work, sacrifice, and financial discipline will eventually have serious payoffs. You'll be socking away cash. You'll be paying down debt. You'll be building up a reserve like a squirrel in winter, considering the wisdom of every financial decision. You'll start to cultivate a life full of travel, adventure and exploration. And before you know it, the tables will turn. You will find yourself not the victim of envy, but the subject of it. Your peers will start to look at your life and all the amazing things that you are able to do, and they will begin to look upon you with awe. It is then that they will understand your motives behind pilfering from the employee fridge. They'll suddenly see the deeper meaning behind all those peanut butter sandwiches. They'll get why you went for the Eight O'Clock Bean instead of the Starbucks. And when they go to stroke that check for their gigantic car payment while you're out surfing in Baja, they just might stop and reconsider their choices too.

Going Full Dirtbag: A practical guide and resources for adventure on the cheap:

Along with the broad philosophical principles we learned in Australia, there are a few battle-tested travel strategies for saving money, particularly when you're traveling in more expensive countries, which can help cut out most major expenses. If you really have no money, don't want to work, or are just a genuine cheapskate, there are some basic, ethical strategies you can use to keep the adventure going. All of these are legal. None of them will typically be the easiest, or most comfortable way to go. That's why they're free. But all of them are things most people can do at least occasionally when dirtbagging.

Accommodation:

This is maybe the easiest one to troubleshoot because the sharing economy is well developed and there are a ton of helpful web tools. Freecampsites.net and Campendium.com are both great free camping wiki resources in the US and Canada for travelers with a car, and we've almost never paid for camping since we found them. They also direct you to a lot of cool, out of the way spots you wouldn't likely find otherwise, and the occasional sketchy rest stop. If you're not camping, some of the best tools for getting (and providing!) free accommodation are Warmshowers.com (an evocatively named network specifically for people who are bike touring) and Couchsurfing.com. Both of those have large networks of participants. Just plan ahead, because it's not as easy as just showing up at the door.

If you're flexible in where you can go, have a lot of time to plan ahead, or you want to be in one spot for a long period of time, you might look into house sitting "professionally" through sites like Trustedhousesitters.com, Mindmyhouse.com, or Caretaker.org (think putting together references and a resume to convince people to let you take care of their place for months at a time while they're gone).

Or in a similar vein, look into work to live programs in hostels or volunteer programs in hiker huts - as in the New Hampshire White system, with the Appalachian Mountain Club, or in the Albergues along the Camino de Santiago.

This only works if you're in New Zealand, but it's still a screamin' deal: a backcountry hut pass there only costs $90NZ at time of writing, and will get you six months of accommodation - although you will typically have to hike to them and move every couple of weeks.

Other accommodation options include camping out at trailheads or along forest service roads in Wilderness or National Forest areas, sleeping in the back of your car at rest stops, casinos or Walmart parking lots, or asking at local churches if you can camp out on their property. All of those are generally legal. Tinted window are great. Don't pee or poop in public parking lots - look for 24 hour places to park to make that less tempting.

And of course, if you're into backpacking, it's a simple solution to just wander into the wilderness and hang out there.

But don't set up your tent on the sidewalk, even if it's late and you're tired. Angel almost got arrested for that in Colorado.

Food

This one is a little trickier and might require a bit more pride-swallowing. Dumpster diving (or "Urban foraging" if you prefer) is always an option, and can be an ethical way to help reduce consumer waste as well as a great money saver. Perhaps safer is asking around at bakeries, groceries and restaurants if they have anything they are going to throw out at closing time. Some have policies against this, but I've seen some skilled Freegans spend a few hours making phone calls to area businesses in a small town, and return with 4 dozen donuts, multiple giant bags of potato chips, and a couple of cakes. Freegan.info is the classic resource. There's also an excellent article on diving for food written by the blogger and dirtbag activist Rob Greenfield at robgreenfield.tv/dumpsterdiving/

Another option is to ask around at food banks or soup kitchens if they will allow you to volunteer there in exchange for a chance to shop. It's generally bad form to pretend to be a local and use those services, because stealing from poor families makes you an asshole, but making yourself useful helps them out and rewards you for your time.

Hygiene

After a long day of dumpster diving, you're going to need a shower. You can buy or build a homemade solar shower for a couple of bucks that'll turn any water source into a serviceable bathroom. Alternately, campsites, truck stops, and hostels will generally have a fee you can pay to shower without staying. Local pools will also have showers you can use if you pay for entry (just don't use the pool itself to bathe). And if you happen to have a membership to a chain gym or YMCA it's a popular option to utilize their resources.

After living outside for a while, you'll probably start to worry less about this anyway - skinny dipping in mountain lakes makes for a pretty serviceable bathing alternative, and <u>not</u> shaving is a great time and money saving alternative to shaving.

Local churches, especially larger ones, will often have laundry machines if you want to skip the laundromat, but once again it's probably unethical not to offer something in return: make yourself useful, do some gardening, offer to help fix something. Don't be a mooch!

Of course, laundry machines are entirely unnecessary and a bucket and scrub brush make for a functional alternative. Or in a pinch, a gallon ziplock and some soap.

Transportation

You could always get a bike or walk. Bike touring and thru-hiking are some pretty sweet and time-honored penniless dirtbag options. So's getting a canoe and floating it down the Mississippi. All that's free if you have the gear.

But if you want to move faster, and you don't have money for a car, you're probably going to have to learn to hitch. There's the classic thumbing it option which works anywhere in the world, but in the US/Canada anyway you can also use sites like Pop Rideshare, Craigslist and rdvouz.com to find someone with a car who'll take you where they're going.

And if you want to fly for free, you can, but you're going to have to plan ahead and be a little bit anal retentive. We don't have anything beyond a frequent flyer account with Alaska Airlines, so I'm nothing like an expert on this, but "Travel Hacking" by signing up with, and proactively managing, frequent flyer and point programs associated with credit cards is a whole underground skill set you can learn online, and can essentially manufacture free money for you, in the form of travel miles. Our friend Six2 paid for all of his flights on an entire round the world trip this way in 2017, so you can definitely use it to get from Florida to Utah, or whatever. "Nomadic Matt" Kepnes is my personal favorite travel blogger on this, and he has a couple of classic budget travel books. "The Ultimate Guide to Travel Hacking" is a great resource, or (more likely because you're a dirtbag) just go to his website, nomadicmatt.com, and search "Travel Hacking". He has a ton of free information. Chris Guillebeau, a guy who visited every country in the world by the time he was 35, is also great on this. Google 'em!

CHAPTER 2: CAREER

In the last chapter we focused on how to manage your financial resources in order to fit as much adventure into your life as possible. This chapter will explore a closely related subject: the means by which you obtain these financial resources.

There are two main areas to explore. The first, is a practical discussion of some common career strategies that people living a life of adventure employ in order to make their dream life possible. The second, is a broader discussion that seeks to explore the concept of career itself. We will examine the ways that people living the dirtbag lifestyle challenge conventional social norms of career and identity, and in so doing, offer up a new, more liberating perspective on the role of work in our lives.

At the end of this chapter, you will find an appendix with additional resources to consult as you're trying to carve out your own career path, from helpful blogs, to actual job postings that will send you on your way.

But to begin, I want to share the story of my "a-ha" moment, when I recognized that living the dirtbag dream is a possibility for everyone, not just sponsored athletes or those with six-figure trust funds. It was the moment that I first realized that it is entirely feasible to organize your work life in a way that will support your dreams of travel and adventure, not detract from them. My hope is that this story will serve as inspiration for you too. I hope that it will put you in the right mindset to absorb the forthcoming material about how people actually do it, and to think about your situation from the aspect of possibility and positivity.

"Just Quit"

In the Autumn of 2013, in front of a small crowd packed in to *Seven Hills*, a trail-focused running shop in Seattle, Heather "Anish" Anderson (who I introduced earlier in this book) gave a talk about her experience setting the overall self-supported speed record for the Pacific Crest Trail, completing the 2,650 mile journey in just 60 days, 17 hours, and 12 minutes.

The presentation focused, as one might expect, on the logistics and details of Heather's success in accomplishing the massive and incomprehensible task of hiking an average of 44 miles a day for 60 days straight. But she also talked about the backstory that prepared her for the experience. She spoke about how, following college, she'd hiked all three of the American long distance trails. She explained how she had tried to settle down after that, but still had a deep thirst for long days out on the trail. She had taken up ultra-running to try and quench her thirst, but it never really worked. So, she decided to drop it all in pursuit of the speed record dream - which she ultimately achieved.

It became clear in that backstory, that for years, Anish had managed to organize her life around big adventures -

repeatedly leaving for months at a time to venture into the woods on long trails. After her presentation, when the floor was opened for conversation, someone in the audience asked a question that was banal, but also on everyone's mind: "How in the world do you get time off from work to do these kinds of things?"

Heather's response was a matter of fact, "Oh, I just quit!" Then she chuckled nonchalantly, as if this was the most natural thing in the world.

At the time of her talk, it had been 10 years since Angel and I had taken our life-changing trip to Australia. While I've pointed to that trip as one of the greatest learning experiences of our lives, the truth is, we didn't exactly spend the years immediately following it living a fancy-free life of grand adventure.

During that period, we managed to do plenty of cool shit - we lived in New Zealand for a couple of years, purchased a condo in a rad neighborhood in Seattle, got into trail running, even worked our way up to running a couple ultras. But we also spent a huge amount of our time working to pay down the significant amount of debt we had accrued. By the time we made it to Heather's talk, I had worked everywhere from bottle warehouses to religious institutions before I eventually went back to school to become a nurse. Angel had worked full-time while also studying to become a nurse practitioner. During most of that period (including our time abroad), both of us were either working two jobs simultaneously, or working on a job and a degree at the same time.

As Heather's words "just quit" reverberated through my brain, it was as if time slowed down. A profound realization had just hit me. Hearing Anish so confidently say, "Just quit" brought to the surface something that I think I had been feeling deep down for a while, but unable to fully express: that I was allowing an outside force (a false one at that), to determine how I spent the vast majority of my time. With this realization, I started to take a whole new look at the philosophy that our culture indoctrinates us into: that spending the bulk of your time at work is your duty, a thing you simply must do if you want to be an adult. Living as I was with these shackles of the mind, how could I ever quit? Quit? No. Never. Quitting is what irresponsible people do. Quitting could put my entire life in jeopardy. I could never do that!

The fact is, this can be a hard idea to swallow. Let's face it, it runs against most of our cultural assumptions about work and what it means to be a "success". And for the record, Anish's "just quit" comment didn't exactly garner a standing ovation. I distinctly remember looking around, observing the way the crowd responded. People were glancing at their neighbors, laughing nervously, bemused and skeptical. I heard at least one person mutter, "Must be nice!"

I'll admit, as powerful as this message was to hear, a part of me felt the same way. As a guy from a midwestern farming community with parents who worked six or seven days a week running their own separate small businesses my entire life, who had hard work and career ingrained in my DNA, the idea that one could just quit their job to do what they wanted seemed somewhat implausible, if not a bit reckless.

But there was also a voice in the back of my head that shouted, "Hell yeah! I'm in!"

Perhaps this spark was there because Heather's comment

came at just the right time in my life. Angel and I were already in transition. I'd just become a nurse, and we'd just retired our student debt. After many years of feeling mired in our work lives, we now had substantial flexibility in our jobs and finances. Ambitions for long-term travel and adventure that had been born in Australia came flooding back, and for the first time in our lives, it seemed like a legitimate possibility to pursue. We were in a third-life crisis of the best kind, and the future seemed full of possibilities.

After Heather's presentation, I knew that our own situation left few excuses for why we couldn't organize a lifestyle like the one that she had. Despite the fact that she was now a world-record holder, before this hike she was totally unknown as an outdoor athlete. She had received no sponsorship, and was so broke that she fueled herself during this amazing feat by eating 17 Clif Bars a day that were left over from a trail race she helped direct, alongside ziplocks filled with a cheap mixture of peanut butter and jelly. And I knew for a fact that she paid for her lifestyle on a service industry wage, because we had frequently stopped in the grocery store where she worked in Central Washington on our way to the mountains. Angel and I were now both employed as nurses with no debt and solid earning potential, so Heather's life begged the question, "If she can do it, why can't we?"

The answer, ultimately, was that we could. While it took the idea a couple of years to germinate, in 2015 we quit our full-time jobs to follow Heather's literal footsteps on the PCT. Following our thru-hike, we traveled for 4 months in Latin America, and spent 6 months drifting around the American West picking up short-term work intermittently while we explored, hiked, and ran to our hearts' content. And 4 years later, we've never gone back to full-time jobs, long-term contracts, or the measly 2 weeks of vacation a year. We still have a lot to figure out, but I think we can say, like Anish, that we've made a lifestyle of it.

From "Must be nice" to "How'd they do that?!"

Heather's message resonated so deeply with Angel and I, because of an instinct that was already deep within us - the sense that our careers were not our calling. When we were living stationary lives in the Seattle area, a big part of why we fell in love with trail running, was that it allowed us to explore huge chunks of wilderness in a short period of time - up to 100 miles in a weekend. While we had spent years advancing our careers, the truth was that our jobs (even if we were generally happy with them) were not what we were most passionate about. What we were most passionate about was travel and exploration.

That sense, I've come to believe, is the heart of the dirtbag identity - the "Dirtbag's Golden Rule" in relation to their career. **A dirtbag, at their core, is someone who finds their calling not in their career path, but in the instinct to explore.** This isn't some novel feeling that appeared in Yosemite Valley in the '50s. It's an expression of a deep-rooted, widespread human instinct that you see reflected in people throughout history - from our ancestral nomads roaming the African plains, to the Polynesians who explored the Pacific without so much as a map and compass.

The instinct to explore has been largely suppressed in modern culture. While explorers and adventurers with serious financial backing have been venerated, it has not been practical for average people living in industrialized economies to strike out and explore regularly. Agriculture and industrialization have made survival largely geographically dependent for most. And even where it has been possible, it hasn't necessarily been socially acceptable. The terms vagabond, drifter, and hobo have historically been used to imply that peripatetic people are dangerous losers, not celebrated members of society.

But in a lot of ways, the world that is now taking shape is opening up possibilities for this type of lifestyle - not just for the Richard Branson's of the world, but for the rest of us. From the gig economy, to the decline of the long-term career path, to the flexibility of online employment and work from home arrangements, the ways that people make money in the 21st century are becoming less location dependent. And that's great news for the intrepid dirtbag.

Average people are now developing strategies to live adventurous lives in the Brave New World. For Angel and I, those people have been the reason that we've been able to continue moving down our current path, following our initial inspiration from Heather. We've encountered hundreds of dirtbags who are figuring it out, both in person, and by proxy on the internet, and we've benefited immensely from the knowledge they've shared with us.

I want to share the stoke, so the rest of this chapter will introduce you to the things we've learned, and the people we've learned from. We'll talk about a variety of career paths that real people have followed that have worked, and we'll discuss different types of life strategies that are available for people who want to maximize the time they have to explore.

I hope that at some point you too will think to yourself, "Must be nice!" While this may sound a bit odd, I would argue that a bit of jealousy is an indicator that you have encountered something that you really want deep down. If you can take the energy in this thought and turn it around, it can actually be quite motivating. Instead of looking at someone in envious fury, you can look at them as inspiration. After all, if they did it, it's clearly possible. If they managed a way to figure it out, so can you. The question then, is "how?" My goal with the rest of the chapter is to give you some practical answers to that.

Career Strategies that Center on Adventure

It's worth stating that while it can be hard to make the philosophical shift from a career centered worldview to an adventure centered worldview, concretely, we aren't actually talking about anything particularly complicated. We're just talking about how you make the time and the money to get out on your chosen adventures.

When you break it down that way, it's helpful because it becomes less daunting. It's just a puzzle. How do I create more time to travel, or surf, or hike, or paddle, or climb, or run while also making enough money to survive?

That keeps career in its place, as a way to get the resources you need to survive.

And it is a nice reminder that there are a million possible options. If one isn't working, you can try another. You're not locked in. People figure it out in a lot of different ways.

The classic dirtbag pattern is to work very little and survive on very little, which we'll talk about more. But there are endless ways that people tackle the problem of centering their life on the outdoors and adventure.

Broadly speaking, we can group these strategies into three categories.

1. Minimize your time spent working by minimizing the amount you spend, or maximizing the amount you make.
2. Find balance with work and adventure.
3. Figure out how to get paid to do what you love.

Now, let's dive in to career strategies that fit into each of those categories.

Strategy 1: To maximize adventure, minimize your time spent working and minimize the amount that you spend.

Our previous chapter on money argued that the heart of the dirtbag ethos is the commitment to go as far as you can with as little as you can, and for that reason, this first set of career paths are the most purely dirtbaggy. They assume full commitment to that cause, and they're focused on living as cheaply as possible in order to work as little as possible.

The Pure Dirtbag

Real dirtbags go further with less all the time. That means that they spend as little as possible both while they're stuck at home earning money, and when they're on the road doing what they want - whether that's climbing, skiing, surfing, running, hiking, sailing, or just drifting down international dusty roads.

But it's also true that classically, a big part of the reason that they're so cautious with money is that they don't have much, because when they work, they work primarily low-paying jobs. Their ideal job is flexible and portable, and requires a low level of emotional investment so that they can spend as much of their energy as possible on their passion. As a result, classic dirtbag jobs are simple, often temporary or seasonal vocations such as, bartending or serving in a restaurant, ski instructing, river guiding, or working in retail. Sometimes, pure dirtbags demonstrate their dedication to the cause by leaving behind a highly-skilled, well-paying position that they spent considerable time and energy training to do, in order to have more flexibility.

Anish exemplified this lifestyle when she was in the process of breaking the speed record on the Pacific Crest Trail, funded on grocery store work and fueled by leftover Clif Bars. To become fully invested as a thru-hiker, she left behind a professional career path in tech, diving head-first into her dirtbag dream.

I also think of "Team UltraPedestrian" Ras and Kathy Vaughan, a Washington couple who are in their 50s now that have spent their whole lives bouncing between jobs - working lifts at ski resorts, gardening, caretaking houses, driving trucks, and I'm sure a whole lot more. Along the way, they've poured their primary energy into dirtbaggy pursuits like pioneering a new thru-hiking route in the Pacific Northwest (the "UP North Loop"), skiing all 200k of groomed trail in the cross country paradise of Mazama, Washington in a single week, and creating the "UltraPedestrian Wilderness Challenge" that inspires others to take up similar adventures in the Pacific Northwest. They refer to themselves as full-time adventurers, and they've lived that way for years on a series of low-paying jobs and side hustles. They have always found a way to make it work. They even managed to raise a kid in the process, who predictably turned out to be a rad world-traveling, ultra-running snowboarder.

The major advantage of this lifestyle is that it is accessible to almost anyone, and it allows you to live fast and free with low levels of responsibility, anywhere in the world. You might have to sacrifice dignity, stability, and future savings, but even a 20-year-old crust punk can figure out how to carve out time for adventure if they are able to avoid spending money at all costs and are willing to work whatever jobs are available.

The major disadvantage is that for most people, it's not sustainable to do this in the long term. One reason these types of pure dirtbags achieve hero status is that the lifestyle is really difficult to maintain for most people. The instability and lack of funds is anxiety provoking, and challenges building long-term relationships and some degree of creature comforts drives most people out of this lifestyle after a couple of years. It's a classic experience to dive into this type of lifestyle with idealistic dreams, grow jaded or exhausted after a few months of living this way, then start to look for ways to get a bit more money and stability than what bagging groceries and sleeping in your car affords. Only the most dedicated do this for years at a time.

But don't let that deter you from trying it for a while. You might find that you've got what it takes, and even if you bow out after six months or a year, it'll be among the most memorable six months or a year of your life.

Resources:

My favorite online profile of Anish, which outlines her transition from relatively normal to full dirtbag really well is the article "A Ghost Among Us" from Backpacker Magazine.

"Not a Chance" is another hiker who exemplifies the dirtbag approach to life, and chronicles it on her hilarious gonzo blog, "As the Trail Turns."

"Team UltraPedestrian" are active on all major social media outlets, but they keep their main online hub at UltraPedestrian.com.

The Dirtbag Rich

There are people who riff on the dirtbag approach, who are equally interested in maximizing their time adventuring and minimizing their time working, but who manage to take some of the stress out of pure dirtbaggery by getting jobs where they make more money. I call them the dirtbag rich.

Fundamentally speaking, the only difference between the dirtbag rich and the pure dirtbag is their earning potential. The dirtbag rich still avoid spending money to the greatest degree that they can, sleep in their cars, and shop at thrift stores so they can spend large parts of their years skiing, surfing, or hiking. They also frequently seem to have just as little interest in being tied down by a desk job as the classic dirtbag. It's just that when they work, they also manage to get jobs that pay professional level wages, so they can make money more quickly, enabling them to work less and take more time off.

I don't know about you, but for me, people doing this trigger the strongest "must be nice" impulse, because it seems that they have the best of both worlds: tons of freedom and little financial anxiety.

The first people I remember meeting who exemplified the "dirtbag rich" were Matt and Julie Urbanski. Their lifestyle initially blew my mind. At first, it was hard for me to wrap my head around what they were able to do. But as time moved on, their lifestyle, and the strategies they employed to facilitate it, became an inspiration that we began to emulate in our own lives.

The Urbanskis were a young couple who started out without much money. Both had studied finance in college, and upon graduation, stepped into nicely paying jobs in the financial sector. They buckled-down, put their noses to the proverbial grindstone, and committed themselves to saving as much of their earnings as possible. They limited their spending, exercised self-discipline, and in just a few years they were able to take 3 years off from work. During this time, they completed the coveted Triple Crown, ran a number of ultras, spent time in Guatemala traveling and learning Spanish, and even wrote three books.

When we met them, they were just settling back in to "ordinary" life for a few years in Seattle to begin the process of replenishing their coffers. We were starting to think about ways we could get more freedom ourselves, so we were immediately intrigued to learn how they were doing it.

What we came to learn is that, even working high-paying jobs, they were extremely disciplined in their spending. They lived like misers in small spaces, drove beat-up cars, and aimed to save 80% of their income, which they invested in accounts that would earn interest but also allow for withdrawals as needed. In short, they were rich people who lived like dirtbags, and it bought them a long period of freedom. And it's worked again: after a few years in Seattle, they're currently drifting around the world raising their kid, trail running, and starting a running coaching business.

It's easy to hear about jobs in finance and immediately jump into the "must be nice" impulse and discount the possibility of replicating this situation in your own life. I know, because that was my initial response to the Urbanskis lifestyle.

But now I believe that this type of lifestyle is actually widely accessible. While it is true that the "dirtbag rich" lifestyle is based upon obtaining a job that requires a deeper commitment to education and work experience, it isn't just for Wall Street Bankers and hotshot lawyers - this approach is replicable with a variety of career paths.

To be clear, becoming "dirtbag rich" doesn't require that you become *actually* rich. If you're living on the cheap, an average income is enough to achieve the dirtbag dream, and most any professional career path will allow you to replicate what Julie and Matt did to some degree.

Like any dirtbag job, the ideal job for the dirtbag rich is portable, sustainable, flexible, and easy to come by. It's a big psychological barrier if you aren't certain you'll be able to replace your job if you leave it for long periods of time. And it's true that if your job isn't both lucrative and easy to come by, this can be an anxiety provoking approach to life. It's also true that the instability and frequent transitions built into this type of lifestyle will create conditions that aren't suitable for everyone. A common theme you'll see repeated in this book, is that living a radical life will often mean making some radical choices. You may have to step out of your comfort zone. You will have to endure some sacrifice. In the end, it's up to you to determine whether these choices are suitable to you or not.

But I really do think that a huge number of ballsy people are already primed to live like the "dirtbag rich." If you are in the middle of your life, and most of your major debts are paid off, you are in a great position to save most of your earnings. Or, if you are in your youth, and life in the capitalist world hasn't yet sucked you in, you can make many empowering decisions to avoid debt and fund a life of adventure.

One of my favorite illustrations of how the dirtbag rich lifestyle can be achieved is found in the couple we introduced you to in the last chapter: Antonio and Karla Martinez. They have been living for years with Antonio splitting time between working as a rafting guide around the world, and maintaining their home base in Mexico. They run a small guiding business in their hometown of Jalcomulco in Veracruz State, but the vast majority of their income has come from guiding abroad. It isn't a high-paying job, but they have been able to fund an entire life in Mexico on short-term contracts for years. (It's worth noting that they are Mexican nationals, but this lifestyle is just as achievable for anyone who wants to spend up to six months at a time in Mexico. Visitors visas are typically hassle-free to obtain).

In English-speaking countries, jobs in healthcare provide one of the classic paths towards this kind of lifestyle. "Travel nursing" or other forms of contract work are a well-known strategy among nurses around the world who want to take short-term contracts that pay well in cool places on short notice, and in our own travels we've met dozens of RNs pursuing this path - in the U.S., New Zealand, Australia and Canada. There are agencies around the world that help with these sorts of job placements, and if you're a licensed RN with location flexibility, you can have a job in a matter of days.

If you are not interested in spending the time and money required to train as a nurse, a vanlifer we met in California named Jess Soco taught us that these types of contracts are also available across the range of medical careers, including technician jobs that require much less investment. At least in the U.S., techs are in high demand in a variety of healthcare fields - including surgery, radiology, mental health, and laboratory work. Many training programs only require a year of study at affordably priced community colleges. Since her kids graduated, Jess has been spending her 40s and 50s in California working six months or so a year as a tech, and the rest of her time hiking, traveling and trail running.

Essentially, any trade where short-term contracts are available can support a similar lifestyle. We met a trucker on the PCT who spent his winters working and his summers hiking. I met a union electrician in Kentucky who traveled Southeast Asia in between jobs. And I've met dozens of tech programmers whose careers are comprised of a series of project contracts interspersed with periods of freedom.

In my experience, most people who have the means to live this way still don't, even if they really want to, and I have some broad hypotheses about why.

One thing preventing people from going this route is fear of the unknown. In North America, taking long periods of time off from work is not something many people have done voluntarily or intentionally, so not many people have a developed a sense of how much it will cost or what is involved. Most people (including me) are by nature risk averse, and we follow the dominant cultural patterns because they're predictable and feel safe. But there are other patterns that are also safe, and when you have stable finances and marketable skills, the "risks" involved with leaving a job are often much less risky than we assume.

A related issue is simply poor planning. When we get into a position where we are making more money than we need, we tend to get addicted to it by developing a lifestyle that depends on that continued cash flow rather than maintaining a cheaper lifestyle and saving the extra. Most people eventually get addicted to the rat race of purchasing clothes, cars, technology, and housing that will match or one-up their peers. That wastes absolutely massive amounts of time and money, and eats up absolutely massive opportunities to do things that are way cooler in life. Most things the average person buys in the English speaking world aren't necessary, and when you redefine "rich" to mean "having more than enough money to cover the basic essentials" most us have the capacity to get rich if we're intentional about it. Maybe not "rich" rich, but "dirtbag rich."

Since employment is such a strong cultural value in the United States, it is also true that there are some particular built-in penalties for taking time off from work. The employment-based medical insurance model is perhaps the most notable, and in some states it is extremely expensive to pay for your own coverage (we'll talk about that more in a bit). Many jobs use positive incentives to retain employees (the Urbanskis talk about regular bonuses in financial institutions as "golden handcuffs" that you have to fight your instincts to reject). And, I've heard rumors that some companies don't see it as a job qualification that you spent a year drifting around Europe skiing. Crazy, right?

But among people who have taken the risk of quitting work to travel, climb, or do whatever they want, I've yet to meet anyone whose life was derailed because of it. They might have had less money, or less job advancement, but they got in more travel, climbing, and doing whatever they wanted in exchange.

Resources:

Check out Matt and Julie Urbanski's helpful blog post on their approach to finances, and follow their lives as they progress on Urbyville.com.

They link to Gocurrycracker.com as one of their favorite financial blogs for people who want to establish a similar lifestyle. I trust them, so I'm including it here too.

And KeepThrifty.com is a great resource created by a couple who call themselves "Dirtbag Millionaires" and explain how they live out the "Dirtbag rich" lifestyle (Despite the similar names, I swear I didn't steal the idea from them - I stole it honestly from the Urbanskis!)

Early Retirement

This is a little beyond the purview of what we're doing here, so I'm not going to dig that deep, but it's worth noting as an aside that early retirement can basically be a variation on the "dirtbag rich" strategy when extrapolated out. It involves working for a long period at as high an income as possible, while living well below your means, so you can eventually quit working altogether and do what you want for the rest of your life - ideally at an age younger than 65.

The main pro of this approach is probably obvious: you get to spend a big chunk of your life doing whatever you want

Perhaps the cons are a little more hidden, but as someone whose father died unexpectedly at a relatively young age after a lifetime of 6 day work weeks, I can attest that they are no less profound. Nothing in life is ever guaranteed, and the long game strategy of working and saving for "someday" can backfire if your health takes a turn, the economy tanks, or disaster strikes. And for a group of readers whose goals involve lots and lots of physical activity, the risks of deferred dreams are even higher. No amount of planning can change the fact that, the older you get, the more likely you'll be to get sick, develop health issues, or die.

As someone who is still relatively young, I don't want to fall into the trap of thinking that my time's unlimited. In general, that's why I'm more about gap years, big trips, and "midlife retirements" which allow you to live out your goals right now, rather than waiting until you're older.

For the readers with significant savings or who are older, early retirement might be a great option, and I hope you can do it. My favorite free online resource on that is the blog "*Our Next Life*," because the authors are financially savvy and do an amazing job of running down the intricacies of how they managed to save and retire at around 40 years old. It's also a helpful resource because they think about retirement in more complex terms than just hanging on a beach somewhere. It's not like they stopped working or being productive. It's just that they found a way to do exactly what they *want* to be doing, rather than what they *have* to do. When you shift from *required* action to *inspired* action, life gets a lot more fun.

The good news is that this approach makes "early retirement" more achievable. From this perspective, "early retirement" doesn't necessarily mean having enough money to survive forever. It just means having enough to be able to spend your time on what you really want instead of grinding away for years at something you hate.

And I would guess that most of you reading aren't actually that interested in completely stopping work at 40, 50, or even 60. But there's a good chance that you do want to escape the feeling that you are shackled to your job. You likely want more freedom. You likely want to find work that supports your lifestyle goals, instead of feeling stuck in something that inhibits them.

I'm reminded of a friend, Tony Epps, who recently "retired" in his early 40s from a naval career. He still wants to be a part of the workforce, so is planning on retraining to become a nurse. He is doing this with a clear intention of being able to work when and where he wants. Before he begins nursing school, he is traveling the world, trail running, and planning for a thru-hike. His goal is to be able to continue travelling like this after earning his credential. He will be able to do so, because he will have established a job with good earning potential and a flexible schedule.

I also think about our friends Tim "Ironhusk" Macauley and his wife Maya, who left their tech jobs in their 40s to turn a passion-project producing handcrafted purses into their primary careers. They did this in order to spend as much time hiking and running as possible. They haven't stopped working, they're just doing exactly the work that they want, while spending more time on their hobbies.

In short, reframing your approach to work can have key benefits. Maybe it's not realistic to quit work altogether. But it is realistic to seek out ways to make it a lot more fun.

Tanja Hester, one of the authors behind Our Next Life, is releasing a book soon called "Work Optional" about this topic. Their other writing has been so helpful that even my cheap ass might buy a copy.

Strategy 2: To minimize the amount that you resent work, make it balance with adventure.

All of the options so far assume that you readers are the type of people who are just trying to get away from your jobs, so we've been focused on balancing the life equation so that time spent on adventure is expanded and time spent working is minimized. I would imagine that may describe a significant portion of you, but I would also imagine that plenty of others are aiming to have it all: ample time spent adventuring, and lots of time spent on a healthy, productive career that will allow a comfortable lifestyle without the stress over which type of cat food will make the best taco filling. A lot of you, I'd guess, don't mind working, but just want something better than a lifetime at work with a week or two of vacation a year.

The good news is that you have options too.

Go Euro Style

It could be that all you really want is a 30 hour work week, plenty of money to live on, a meaningful career, and a couple of months off every summer to go on some grand excursions. You want to hack life's equation and have it all - make lots of money and still have time to do everything you want. For many of you that might seem unattainable, but for one group it's not: Europeans.

Maybe it seems crazy or unimaginable for some, but for those of you American readers looking for the perfection of work/life balance, the elegant solution might be to consider leaving the country. It seems to me that America keeps trying to jump the shark in a thousand different ways anyway. If you're a professional, why not start looking into jobs abroad? Many European countries offer substantially more annual leave than the United States, making it not only less weird, but more possible to spend more time on your passions. New Zealand, Australia, Singapore or dozens of other options are also good possibilities.

But for those who aren't interested in jumping ship, there are a variety of ways of establishing a Euro-style existence in North America, even if it's not the standard path in most fields.

When we spent a month on the Camino de Santiago a few years back, the disproportionate number of American teachers we met was a nice reminder that working within the education system provides some great perks for people who want to spend a significant portion of their life unencumbered by work. It's true that teachers earn those summer vacation hours during the grind of the school year, but the educational system is one employment option where extended periods of freedom are built in. A variety of jobs within schools and universities follow a seasonal schedule with summers off, so it's worth remembering that this schedule is available for support staff and administrative professionals as well.

Other seasonal jobs can offer similar benefits. A few quick examples that come to mind are: ski patrollers, wilderness firefighters, hospitality workers, and tax professionals. Each of these professions make it possible to build a seasonal career where you can enjoy long periods of time off.

I'm not an employment expert, and I won't pretend to be, but because we hang out with vagabonds and dirtbags, Angel and I have met people who've managed to incorporate a ton of freedom into a variety of career paths - truckers, business consultants, accountants, techies, doctors, nurses, hospital techs, construction workers, the list goes on. A basic point that I've come to believe is that if you have a skill that helps people, then you can figure out how to get paid for it in both short-term positions and long-term careers. And the further you get into your career, the more true this is.

And a final pro-tip, whatever your career: You might actually already *have* more flexibility in your job than you realize. If you're in a job that you like, but are considering quitting because you want more time off, tell your company that before resigning. A lot of life is determined by what you ask for, and your job may well want to figure out what it will take to keep you. They might have options for sabbaticals, part-time arrangements, or leaves of absence that will work for what you want. You never realize how much power and influence you have in your job until you tell them that you're thinking of quitting.

Flexjobs.com is a well-regarded online resource for people looking for work on non-traditional schedules across career *fields. A thing to bear in mind - their site costs money to join! About $15/month at time of writing. But based on reviews, the fee is worth it because they filter out any chance of getting scammed, and help you drill down exactly to the types of jobs that you may be qualified for. I'm typically against paying for things you don't need to, but this site seems like it's worth it if you're serious about flexible or online work.*

Become a Digital Nomad

The internet may be ruining everything good and sacred in the world, but it has also made it possible for a huge number of people whose job is computer-based to work outside of a traditional office. So, a lot of people are able to collapse the "time spent working" versus "time spent adventuring" equation because their work is location-independent and they are able to do it while they're on the road. They have real careers, and make real money, while posting up in amazing places or drifting from town to town as they please. So you're still working, but you're also constantly adventuring.

Living in the tech-centric Pacific Northwest, this lifestyle is visible everywhere, and I'm super jealous of my friends who can essentially go to work wherever they can find a wifi connection. A couple of our friends, Noa and William, have worked their way up the career ladder at Microsoft, and work a ton of hours, but do so while travelling the world. Their Instagram feed is a constant source of inspiration and deep, deep jealousy.

When we entered the thru-hiking world, we realized that this type of lifestyle was a real possibility outside of the field of tech. On the Camino, we met a woman who was working a few hours a week along the way, who told us that she'd been employed for years as a private bookkeeper. She's able to do this because almost all of her work can be done right on her laptop. She has been traveling the world, working on beaches from Thailand to Australia. When we met her, she was taking a quick work stop at a cafe in Northern Spain.

Internet-based work is expanding across career fields, so the possibility of location independence is becoming feasible for the masses. In healthcare, jobs offering video and phone-based consultations are becoming increasingly common. In journalism and written content production, web-based freelancing has become more the rule than the exception. In education, online tutoring is an increasingly viable career path. In entry-level customer service, Amazon alone hires enough work-from-home employees to populate a small country.

And entrepreneurs have endless low-cost online startup options. The possibilities are as broad as the career paths themselves. Angel and I are essentially trying to establish this model with *Boldly Went*. And our aforementioned role models Matt and Julie Urbanski are setting up a location independent business as running coaches through *Team RunRun*. If you have a skill, it's likely that you can market it to people online.

Journohq.com is a travel blog with a nice run-down on places to get started looking for work as a digital nomad, at an entry level.

Flexjobs is, once again, a great place to start if you're looking for an actual job in your career field.

And pro tip: based on a bit of research and a personal tip from a friend who's done it, Search Engine Evaluation is a commonly *available job that typically earns ~$15/hour and can be done from home without many qualifications. That's plenty to survive on in lots of places in the world, so if you're an international traveler, you could do worse.*

Strategy 3: Maximize adventure by getting paid to do it.

They say that if you do what you love, you'll never work a day in your life, so we should just get to the point that I'm pretty sure you've all been thinking about: you can collapse the whole life equation by figuring out how to combine "time spent working" with "time spent adventuring" by just getting a job outside. Sometimes it's easier to stop finagling to adjust your work life so that your adventure life fits, and cut to the chase finding work that pays for you to do the things you want.

Work Outside

Probably every one of us has daydreamed about getting a cool job that allows us to be outside every day, and for those of us who've never done it, sometimes it's important to have the reminder that it's actually a realistic possibility. Working outside is a real thing that people do, and you can do it too. People pursue entire careers as paddling guides, field biologists, rangers, conservation workers, smoke jumpers, ski instructors, trail running coaches and countless other professions that allow you to get paid to do the things you love.

A principle that I was reminded of recently was that, if you aren't happy with the direction your life is headed, a reasonable first step is to change directions, and get on a ladder you *want* to climb - even if it's just the bottom rung.

While running our own side hustle guiding hikes for travelers staying at City Hostel in Seattle, we met a guy named Max who was in town from France. While chatting with him we asked him what he did for a living. While he'd come from a conventional business background, he told us that a few years back he'd gotten bored with office work and decided to make a major change. He looked around online until he found an organization called *Backroads* that was hiring guides. He was an avid cyclist, and they were an active travel agency that takes small groups on extended biking and hiking trips around the world. He got the job, and ever since, he's been paid a decent wage to do what he wants to do anyway - travel, bike, and explore the world.

While Max might seem like a unicorn, it's worth remembering that if you've been pursuing a passion, you have developed skills that will be valuable to others - whether that is expertise in a particular outdoor pursuit, foreign language skills, knowledge of other countries, or just a high level of physical fitness. Any of those things create a variety of possibilities to get paid for your experience. Whatever your passion, it's worth considering how all that time you've spent doing what you love has been something like an unpaid internship - a set of experiences where you have cultivated the raw skills that employers in many fields are looking for.

For many people considering a career change, starting out by finding a part-time job that sounds appealing, or starting up your own side hustle that allows you to get paid to do the things you love anyway, is a great, low-risk way to start. Most outdoor photographers and writers start out as freelancers, building up a portfolio before taking it on full time. And it's relatively easy to test the waters of guiding either with an existing organization, or by establishing your own small business. English tutoring is a skill that you can be practiced part-time both online and through local agencies, and can open up career possibilities around the world. And putting yourself out there as a coach in whatever area you are most passionate and knowledgeable about can lead to a source of extra income.

<u>Move your work somewhere you love</u>.

Finally, if all of those other strategies fail - if you can't save enough to quit your job, if you can't find a job that gives you lots of time off, if you can't find a job online, or if you can't find a job paying you to do what you want - you can still find a job somewhere cool. It's an unfortunate reality that there will be times when making money has to outweigh other concerns. So, if you have to work, and if all else fails, why not get a job somewhere cool?

In some career paths, it's easier to find jobs than others, of course. But there are thousands of jobs across every field that are within striking distance to amazing outdoor recreation. If you feel stuck and want to get outside more, why not start a job search in one of those places? Even if you only have one day off a week, if you can spend it hiking, climbing, surfing, trail running or skiing, it goes a long way towards feeling okay about your life. We'll talk about this a bit more in the next section on responsibilities, but "weekend warrior" is an honorable title for anyone whose financial realities preclude more thorough outdoor immersion. So, if nothing else works, there's always the option to just move.

Conclusion: You can figure this shit out

None of the career paths I described are standard, and none of them just "happen."

If you're young, or in debt, you realistically might have to pay some dues to balance a degree of freedom with a level of financial stability that prevents money from completely consuming your emotional energy.

If you're older, enmeshed mid-career, have a house, a family, responsibilities - you realistically have to deal with those things, and "just quit" might not be as immediately feasible.

But the thing that I hope comes through is that it's not impossible to integrate huge amounts of adventure into your life if you plan for it, regardless of your life situation.

The dirtbag's most important life lesson: in wealthy societies, a life of adventure is accessible to the majority of people if they're willing to sacrifice for it, and if they're willing to do it on the cheap. You can focus less on making money and more on organizing the life you want if you decide to, because most people in the English-speaking world can make more money than they need to survive.

I know I'm saying this as a person with a lot of privilege, and that I'm glossing over the challenges a lot of people face.

I also know, on the flip side, that I've seen people with some pretty serious challenges figure out some pretty cool shit - blind triathletes, Bolivian world travelers, one-legged ultrarunners, female Eritrean thru-hikers, old and fat and seriously mentally ill pilgrims on the Camino. I don't want to minimize, but *even less do I want to count people out.* Human beings may be a bunch of feral primates pretending to be civilized, but they are also amazingly adaptable. Passionate people figure things out in a variety of situations. The possibilities for all of us are extensive.

Resources to get you started.

The first step is always the hardest, but when it comes to making a career change, these resources will make it easier.

Get professional direction from someone who's done it

I used to be a huge skeptic about life coaching, but when Angel and I made our major shift away from full-time work in traditional jobs into a dirtbaggy existence of travel and adventure and making a living doing things we're excited about, coaching was instrumental. Figuring out what to do with your life is hard because every person's skills, passions, and situation are different. A coach's job is to help you identify your own and figure out how to make them all fit together in a life that's satisfying. In other words, they're professionally trained to get to know you personally and help you get your shit together in a way that makes you happy.

If you're interested in talking individually with someone about making a career or life change, I personally recommend getting in contact with Rob Zimmerman, at www.findyourinnercompass.com.

He was my go to consultant on this book, and is an excellent resource on the dirtbag dream life, because he's gone through it. He quit his career path on the East Coast a few years back and started building a dirtbaggy DIY existence in Tahoe more focused on carving fresh pow than buying new stuff. As part of that process, he's trained professionally as a coach to help other people make similar big changes.

Get a Job

If you're ready to dive in and get to work, there are plenty of great online resources to help you find a new career.

For interesting job postings in general - jobs outside, jobs in cool places, adventure jobs, National Park jobs, travel jobs, guiding, and more - check out Cooljobs.com and Coolworks.com.

If you're interested in non-traditional schedules and employment structures, Flexjobs.com is the recognized go-to resource.

For getting started as a digital nomad, search for an article on the Journo blog, titled "Jobs for Digital Nomads," which includes great links and advice on how to find entry level work.

One of my favorite travel bloggers, Nomadic Matt, wrote the most helpful article I've read about "Finding Work Overseas". It includes advice on the easiest types of work to find abroad, and how to establish yourself in a professional career in another country. Search that one out on nomadicmatt.com.

Set up a Side Hustle

I should give more attention to the topic of "side hustles" - the emerging trend in American life of figuring out strategies outside of our main careers for making money. Our first major intro to side hustling as a lifestyle came when we were travelling in Latin America, where in many countries people don't have "hobbies" so much as multiple jobs, some of which they enjoy more than others. You could read the fact that this a popular trend in the U.S. as a sign of the decline of the empire, and a rebranding of having to work a second job in order to make ends meet. Just as #vanlife is maybe a hip way of talking about having to live in your car, maybe promoting side hustles is just a way to breeze over the fact that the rich are eating the poor in the United States.

But whatevs - I'm not here to make you feel bad about reality. Setting up a side hustle can also be a fun way to come up with strategies to make money off of side projects that you wanted to work on anyway. Personally, I can't knock them because this book and Boldly Went are both examples of side hustles.

The possibilities for making money are infinite. For ideas, I like Chris Guillebeau's "Side Hustle School" podcast as a place to start. He's an interesting dude who spent his 20s travelling to every country in the world, and figured out how to make a living side hustling along the way. He seems genuinely interested in helping other people do the same.

"Desk to Dirtbag," which is written by a guy who's making a living on multiple small projects, also has a useful Side Hustle Calculator aimed to help you figure out how far income from a side hustle might go if you want to use it as a way to extend time off of work to travel, among other things. He also has a good post with 42 ideas for side hustles to stoke your imagination.

Health Insurance

According to leading researchers, the American healthcare system is some bullshit. One manifestation of that bullshit is that, if you are American, and are planning to take long periods of time off from work, or leave a traditional career structure, insurance coverage can be a major barrier because it is so often connected to work and income.

There are, however, a few pro-tips that can make life a little bit easier. First off, if the system is going to play you, you might as well play it back. Some U.S. states are better than others when it comes to access to affordable coverage, and if you're going to move around anyway, it's worth establishing residency in a state where you'll be able to access affordable insurance. This takes some planning - six months to a year, depending on the state - but it comes with big long-term payoffs because living in a state with broad Medicaid coverage and significant subsidies for low income residents makes maintaining insurance coverage much more realistic when you aren't working. Being residents of Washington State, where if you don't earn an income, you are covered by Medicaid for free, was a lifesaver when we took a year off to travel and I needed to see a specialist when I thought I caught a weird jungle disease in South America. (Good news - it was a false alarm!)

Healthcare.gov has a great tool for determining which states offer the best subsidies for low income residents. It's designed to help people who are applying for Medicaid or the Children's Health Insurance Program, but you can also use it to determine which state might provide the best opportunities for you to live the life you want in the long term. Simply go to the site and enter your estimated income level and the state you're interested in moving to. It will tell you whether you'll be eligible for subsidies there, and how much those subsidies might be.

(If you feel like that's abuse of the system, I don't buy it. The system's abusing you, and healthcare should be a right anyway. It's been scientifically proven that the U.S. is a rich country that can afford it, but is full of assholes who choose not to. Okay, sorry. I'll calm down.)

It's also worth noting that one of the many advantages of spending regular time abroad is that travel insurance for health coverage is way cheaper than domestic, because there's nowhere in the world that comes close to the United States' exorbitant healthcare costs. There are a lot of countries where visitors are covered for emergency services regardless of whether they have travel insurance, but better safe than sorry in this instance, because travel insurance is dirt cheap relative to American coverage plans.

World Nomads is an popular insurer, and for the hardcore dirtbag, they have specific coverage for adventure sports. If you aren't going to be doing anything crazy, Atlas, Allianz, and IMG are reliable insurers with cheaper plans.

CHAPTER 3: RESPONSIBILITIES

To jump back to the Anish story, and the "must be nice" impulse, I believe that the instinctual reaction that "one can't just up and leave, Heather," is about more than just money. It's also about the sense that there are things in life that you have to do - family things, work things, house things, or community things. There are "shoulds" in life, and we aren't free to adventure whenever we want. We have *responsibilities*!

I get that. I feel that myself all the time.

Angel and I have been out of the traditional career/house/kid trajectory for years, and if I'm honest, I don't always *feel* good about our decisions. I feel, at some level, that the life I'm living right now is *irresponsible*. We're covering our expenses, paying for health insurance, and (to paraphrase one of my favorite authors, David Quammen) my overall impact on global affairs hasn't noticeably diminished. But still, I *feel* like we should be grinding away at real jobs like everyone else - not leaving money on the table, and not running off to play in the woods when there's work to be done in the city.

That feeling, for a lot of us, is persistent, and as I've tried to identify factors that hold people back from living the lives they dream about, it's come up as a theme again and again. "I can't do that, I have other responsibilities" is an idea that's encountered in every corner of outdoor culture, and I've heard it in multiple conversations about the type of lifestyle we've been talking about here.

But a realization that I've come to across time is that living the dirtbag lifestyle *should* feel irresponsible. And maybe we just need to embrace that.

I don't say that because I think being a dirtbag *is* irresponsible - quite the opposite in fact. But it *is* a way of living that directly critiques traditional definitions of what "responsibility" actually means. And if you're rejecting traditional norms that we're programmed to accept as true, of course it's going to feel weird.

So in order to talk about how to deal with "responsibilities", we have to get right to the heart of the assertion that a "dirtbag" isn't just a smelly climber sleeping on a pile of old blankets in a van. "Dirtbag" is also a full-fledged counter culture, and an alternative lifestyle that requires breaking down traditional notions of what responsibility is. It requires redefining the "shoulds" in life.

And to defend our counterculture against the notion that what we're promoting here is irresponsible, this chapter's Golden Rule is that for dirtbags, **exploration is the most definitive "should". Exploration *is* a responsibility.** It's that assertion that shapes us as an actual counter-cultural movement, and gives us the moral energy to keep going.

There are dozens of reasons that I've come to believe these things are true, and in this chapter, we'll turn our focus to those ideas.

What is a responsibility?

First things first, to make sure we're all on the same page, we should be clear about definitions. When I say "responsibility," I'm referring to something in life that you're obligated to do. It's a debt you owe, or a relationship that you have to maintain, or a vow you have to keep. As Google says, it's having a duty to deal with something.

Defining the term is simple enough. but as every philosopher or parent of a teenager knows, explaining *why* people are obligated to do a thing is much more difficult than telling them that they *are* obligated to do it. I have a Masters Degree in Religion, and I can tell you that there is genuinely no consensus on this stuff.

Pragmatically, there are some legal obligations like contracts and laws that (generally speaking) people agree upon because life will be better for everyone if we all fulfill them. Don't steal and shit. Don't default on your loans. Don't drive drunk. Don't murder people.

And there are moral obligations that seem pretty solidly instinctual - they're the ways that evolution has shaped us to behave, and they work pretty well to keep us from dying. The classics like, "don't go back on your word," or "better take care of yourself" fit this category in some way or another, I think.

But beyond this, there are also a huge number of "responsibilities" - things that people feel that they should do - which are driven primarily by social expectations.

In fact, I would argue that people most commonly feel obligated to do things because of an ingrained acceptance of social standards, and they unthinkingly assume a need to live up to them. This is why people feel responsible, for instance, to have a big house in which to raise their children, even if it isn't essential, because to do otherwise violates a societal standard of good parenting. But many of these standards exist as arbitrary features of culture - not adaptive rules that help us live better, happier lives.

Redefining the "shoulds"

Every countercultural movement, at some point, runs into conflict with the concept of "responsibility". But influential countercultures - from the rock n' rollers to the beatniks to the hippies to the punks - are never exactly about rejecting the idea of "responsibility" outright. They don't say that life has no rules, or that you don't own anything to your fellow humans. They just run into the tension between responsibilities that are legitimate, and ideas that are accepted by mainstream culture as obligatory, but actually aren't. And eventually, countercultures develop their own redefinitions of responsibility, and critiques of common assumptions about what the "shoulds" of life actually are.

Going back to the Chouinard quote stated in the beginning of this book, in important ways, every counterculture says "this sucks" as they vow to live life in a different way. And the assertion of every counterculture worth its salt is that a fair number of the "shoulds" of life are arbitrary at best, and destructive at worst.

And this has been true of dirtbag culture from the very

beginning. As Sara Fleming pointed out in her article, "Because We're Insane" in *Cipher Magazine,* the earliest dirtbags set up camp in Yosemite not just because they loved climbing, but as an explicit rejection of the 1950's American Dream of a house in the suburbs with a white picket fence.

"Dirtbag culture," writes James Plunkett in an essay for *The Good Men Project*, "is a conscientious objection to the so-called American dream of 'Work your ass off, pay taxes and then die.'"

By choosing to split from the norms of society, dirtbags have been implying since the beginning that something within the system is inadequate, maybe even fundamentally wrong, and that there must be a better way.

I can't speak for the founders of the movement, but today we have plenty of evidence that dirtbags are right. The standard path represented by the modern American Dream isn't exactly bearing the fruit that it once promised. Increasing rates of stress-related illnesses, depression, anxiety, burnout, even rage and violence, seem to tell a different story. Instead of making things better, it could easily be argued that this way of living is making things worse, not only degrading our quality of life, but our environment as well.

So the dirtbag critique can be seen as a rejection of many of the "shoulds" that point people toward the illusion of the white picket fence, and the dirtbag lifestyle has been developed as a potentially better alternative.

How does one live as a responsible dirtbag?

As far as I know, no one has ever attempted to examine the dirtbag critique of mainstream culture in depth. No one has attempted to make a list of the ethical precepts of dirtbaggery, and there's no outdoor Pope to define our doctrine from on high.

I haven't tackled the issue with academic precision myself, but, what the hell? I've spent enough time with you people in the last few decades to absorb a few things. I'll give it a shot to get the conversation started, and try to answer the question about what dirtbags are saying about "responsibility". What does a dirtbag say is wrong with the world? And what do they say that you *should* do with your life, and why?

This is all based on my own experience of life in the outdoor community, so you can decide for yourself if this resonates. But to start us off, it is my impression that all of the following are among the mainstream "responsibilities" that are commonly critiqued, or rejected outright, as dirtbags try to figure out the best way to live our lives.

For the dirtbag:

1) You're not responsible to achieve any specific standard of housing or work or financial status. Outdoor culture, in general, feels that prioritization of these types of status symbols is arbitrary and leads to an unhealthy, unfulfilling lifestyle.
2) You're not responsible to be tied to one place for your lifetime. We're all explorers. Some of us stay more local than others. But if you're called to explore, it's better to follow that than to feel tied down by loyalty to town or country.
3) You're not responsible to spend your life suffering to be productive. Because "productivity" is a construct that a)

doesn't have a meaningful definition, and b) usually focuses on making more money to buy more things.

4) You're not responsible to spend your life making money for someone else. Loyalty to an employer is great as long as you're excited about their mission. But if you're just trying to make a living, your level of obligation to yourself, and to the world, should be higher than to some company.

5) You're not responsible to have a nice car or clothes. If you like pretty things, more power to you, but pursuing shiny things is a waste of time and money for the vast majority of us.

6) You're definitely not responsible to go into debt or work overtime to buy crap that you don't need or want. The Joneses don't need to be kept up with. None of us need to waste our lives accumulating things for social reasons. It's unethical to do so, in fact, in a world that's drifting towards overpopulation and is already swimming in its own garbage and waste.

The overall spirit of the dirtbag critique is that life is not meant to be spent merely producing and accumulating things, but rather, thinking critically, exploring the world of possibilities, and engaging actively with our environment. The dirtbag lifestyle is a declaration of independence from the tyranny of consumer culture and the mindless waste of "productivity".

And it's no surprise that one of the biggest appeals of "dirtbagging" is the sense of freedom that comes along with that kind of attitude. Stuff and money don't own you. The rat race isn't mandatory. It's a totally justifiable protest if you decide to smash a copy machine and drive off into the proverbial sunset. Climb all day if you want. Hike your life away. It's more ethical than the mainstream alternative.

But what are we for?

Even if most of us do reject those mainstream cultural assumptions, the dirtbag ethos is not just about saying "this sucks," and the lifestyle isn't primarily about negativity towards the way the world is. In Chouinard's terms, it's about the commitment to do our own thing. It's about defining our own "shoulds,", and crafting our statement about what it means to live a good life.

All of the positive assertions we make, I believe, relate back to the dirtbag's core calling to *exploration*, and this is why I believe that exploration should be viewed as our Golden Rule and our fundamental responsibility. We're the ones charged with the necessary human task of striking out, finding new places, and discovering new possibilities. *Exploration* - even if it is typically driven more by a desire for excitement and adventure than a sense of duty or obligation - is the gift we bring to the world.

That process of discovery, in itself, is important, and we'll return to it to discuss some reasons why in the upcoming chapter on "Finding Meaning". But in the bigger picture, the value of the subculture's commitment to exploration also has to do with the type of people that it creates, and the type of ideas it reinforces. Again, it's true that there's no Pope in the outdoor religion, but there are observable, positive values that have formed in dirtbag culture as a direct result of the lifestyle of exploration that dirtbags have been cultivating for the last 60 years. These are the things we would identify as real "responsibilities" - the actual, legitimate "shoulds" of the dirtbag lifestyle. While they haven't normally been stated explicitly in definitions of what it means to be a dirtbag, they are themes that pop up repeatedly.

What are they? I'm glad you asked, because even if this isn't an exhaustive list, I can think of at least a few:

1) Environmentalism

"You have a whole life in the outdoors, you realize you have a sense of responsibility to protect these wild places." – Yvon Chouinard, *180° South*.

While not everyone who starts skiing or climbing or trail running thinks of themselves as an environmentalist, a whole lot of us end up there. Because environmentalism is essentially about love.

There's a reciprocal relationship between love of the outdoors and time spent there. The longer you're in a place, the more connected you feel to it. And the more connected you feel to a place, the more you're drawn back to it.

Love of place is a huge driver of why dirtbags engage in the activities we do, and it is also a huge driver of the choice to take responsibility for those places. We explore because we love the places where we are and because we're looking for new places to love. And once we find them, it's natural to want to protect them. It's why John Muir founded the Sierra Club, and why it's become standard to see climbers with well-worn copies of *The Monkeywrench Gang* tucked away amidst their rope and carabineers.

So the dirtbag lifestyle of prioritizing outdoor pursuits leads naturally (if not universally) into an environmentalism driven by love of place.

2) Re-humanization in the face of technological advance.

While I don't think dirtbagging leads you to become a Luddite necessarily, immersion in the outdoors for long periods of time does remind you that *homo sapiens* are part of, and dependent upon, their natural environment. And as a result of that awareness, we're also in-tune with what we're losing and perverting with trends towards technology and man-made environments that create walls between humanity and nature, replacing actual experiences with artificial ones. So we push back against it in favor of what we could call "re-humanization".

As people who propel ourselves outside with the power of our own two feet, we're acutely aware of the relationship between activity, health, and feeling human. At some level, being personally responsible includes figuring out how to build a world where humans can do what humans are built to do - which includes using our bodies to move around outside. It's amazing how when we get moving and get healthy, our bodies get stronger and more naturally resilient. We begin to recognize the illusion that human bodies are problems to be solved and controlled. I'm not trying to discount the many marvels that have come with modern technological advancements, but technology is not the all-powerful force that some would like us to believe. There is an *incredible* amount of technology already built-in to the natural world that surrounds us. The core endeavor of dirtbag existence - living and playing outside as much as possible - opens our eyes to that *natural* technology, and exposes the limitations of human-made technology, on a daily basis.

3) Simplicity

Dirtbagging, more than any other lifestyle, is a natural fit with simple, sustainable living because by going as cheap and light as possible, you consume as little as you possibly can. And living out of a backpack, van, or the trunk of a car for long periods of time actually trains you to prefer that lifestyle, and not to see it as a sacrifice.

While a lot of environmentalist lifestyle choices can feel like stoic rejections of comfort done in the name of what's right, it's a common experience among thru-hikers and world travelers to return home from a long trip and throw out a bunch of their stuff - not because of some new ethical commitment, but because they've spent months living without it, and just don't want to have to cart a bunch of crap around. Simplicity becomes, not just a moral stand, but a pragmatic choice made for the sake of comfort and a sense of liberation.

Hand-in-hand with our responsibility to take care of the precious environment that we love and that sustains us, we're responsible to live simply. The dirtbag experience teaches us that life is better that way anyway.

4) Humanism

As with love for wild places, one of the dynamics that just sort of happens with exploration, is that your sense of who's human and who's not expands. When you come into contact with a range of people who aren't like you, and particularly when you rely on them to be your guide, or belay you, or get you down a river, you stop being afraid of people who are different from you, learn to trust them, and expand your own sense of humanity. To riff on Chouinard again, after a life lived relying on a bunch of people who initially freaked you out, you realize that you have a responsibility to protect other humans.

It's important to be cautious here and say that this impulse isn't necessarily automatic. There are plenty of examples of "explorers" who are also shitbags - from cholera-blanket-bearing colonizers, to modern Everest climbers acting like douches to the Sherpas who drag their asses up the mountain.

Most people don't try to be shitbags. At some level, developing affection for people you come into contact with is a standard human response, particularly when you do hard things together. But a lot of times our impact is still shitbaggy, because of the butterfly effect and the unpredicted consequences of good intentions. When we come into contact with new people, they also come into contact with us, and with all of our flaws and misconceptions.

While this dynamic is hard to overcome, it's true that people are getting better at navigating it, at least in some circles, and dirtbags, in many cases, are at the forefront. Broadly speaking, one of the basic dynamics of human interaction is that partnership is the best way to be sure that multiple parties in a relationship benefit equally, and the trend towards immersive travel, and away from resort experiences, is in my opinion, an example of a way that this idea is becoming more of a consensus.

Conclusion

It's probably inevitable that if you identify yourself as a "dirtbag," average people are going to assume that you're not the most responsible person in the world. And it's probably inevitable that you'll internalize some of that.

But I hope the message that's come through here is that it just isn't true. Dirtbags *are* responsible human beings, and in fact may be more conscious about their responsibilities than most. They are, in fact, a counterculture that is defined - like all countercultures - by the attempt to re-imagine what it means to be a responsible human being, and to re-consider all of life's "shoulds." They're taking a proactive approach to constructing a life well-lived, in a way that is not only rare, but is admirable.

It's true - dirtbags insist that a lot of traditional "responsibilities" actually aren't - nice cars and big houses, "productivity", loyalty to employers, and social status, for instance. But they're replacing those misguided pursuits with things that are more valuable - *actual* responsibilities like environmentalism, maintaining our humanity in a over-technologized world, a life of simplicity, humanism, and above all exploration.

We don't have a Pope, but these values are being shaped at a grassroots level by the remarkable individuals who make up the dirtbag community, who are not just shredding gnar, but are building a better world in the process.

Resources, or, Where my definition of responsible dirtbags came from

While the list of dirtbag values in this chapter is my own, I didn't make it up whole cloth. In our own travels, a few people and organizations have been particularly influential in shaping my own understanding of what it means to be a good, responsible dirtbag. Because I want you to have some positive role models as well, I'm providing some examples here. This list is by no means exhaustive, but it is representative of the individuals and organizations who exemplify the values we've been discussing and have helped shape the narrative about what it is, exactly, that dirtbags stand for.

Environmentalism

Ken Campbell, *of Tacoma, WA, is an old school salty dog. He built a career as a kayak guide, lives in an actual sea shanty, and is one of the most knowledgeable paddlers in the Pacific Northwest, having written multiple kayaking guides for the area.*

In 2012, as an outgrowth of his love for the sea, he started a non-profit called "The Ikkatsu Project" in order to raise awareness and conduct research about marine debris, particularly plastics in marine environments. ("Ikkatsu" is a Japanese word meaning "united as one," and his website explains that this is a reference to the sense of connectedness that arose from finding debris from a Japanese tsunami on Pacific beaches in the U.S.)

His work with the project is varied and professional, but Ken's marketing instincts are quintessentially dirtbaggy. Two of his major awareness-raising projects involved gathering trash he found in the water, using it to build boats to paddle in public events. His first effort was the focus of a film called "Message in a Plastic Bottle", in which he constructed a fully functioning kayak out of discarded plastic bottles, and paddled it the 150 mile length of Puget Sound. And in 2018, as part of the inaugural Seventy48 - a 70 mile race between Tacoma and Port Townsend, at the northern tip of the Olympic Peninsula in Washington, he constructed his boat from styrofoam that had washed up on the beach near his house.

Erica Prather, who me met in Denver, but drifts all over, is a pink haired eco-warrior who refers to herself as an "Artivist" because she uses art and media to make a social impact on environmental issues. She's done work with the environmental nonprofit Rocky Mountain Wild, and helped to create the Wild I-70 audio tour - a downloadable audio tour that introduces listeners to the wildlife and environments that make up the 144 mile stretch of Interstate 70 that passes through the Rockies between Golden and Glenwood Springs Colorado.

Like Ken, she's a professional, but she's also a total dirtbag who spends her free time on DIY environmental media projects, including producing "The Cardboard Chronicles" - a YouTube video where she takes a life-sized cutout of Donald Trump on a guided tour of Bears Ears National Monument in Utah. She's also the creator of the Sacred Rage podcast, where she hosts smart interviews with sciency types that tackle complex environmental issues in accessible ways.

Re-Humanization

We introduced "**Team UltraPedestrian**" **Ras and Kathy Vaughan** previously as true lifestyle dirtbags who've managed to finance an adventurous existence for years on side jobs and penny-pinching, but they are also the most vocal proponents I know of, surrounding the idea that playing outside helps us to connect with our humanity in an increasingly dehumanizing world.

On their website, UltraPedestrian.com, and on social media, a constant theme is the idea that we're all bipeds, mammals, and hominids, even if that's an easy thing to forget in our tech-centric world. Maybe owing to their devoted Rastafarian faith, they're as philosophical about their outdoor pursuits as anyone you'll find, and they approach it with real spiritual purpose. As Ras stated in a characteristic quote from an Instagram post:

> "My intent is to reconnect with my ancient Biped and Hominid roots, to take those ancient steps, think those ancient thoughts, and feel those ancient impressions. The illusions of modern society are never more obvious than when perceived with an Ancient Mind."

Chevon Powell is a middle aged African American woman, and if that strikes you as unusual for an outdoor enthusiast, you wouldn't be alone. After being pulled over on her way to an overnight backpacking outing, and hassled by police who didn't believe that someone like her would be doing something like that, she was inspired to start "Refuge Outdoor Festival" in 2018.

The only camping festival specifically organized for people of color in the United States, Chevon's goal with Refuge is to create community, visibility and representation for POC in outside pursuits. A former REI employee and avid hiker, Chevon has organized her whole life around the outdoors, particularly *passionate about pushing back against the idea that the outdoors is "white people shit." And she's had some success. In the first year the festival gathered 125 people from around the U.S. and received both local and national media attention for the cause.*

Simplicity

Marinel de Jesus, *aka "Brown Gal Trekker" quit her job as a lawyer in Washington, DC to pursue a simpler life outside, run a trekking company called Peak Explorations, and write about issues of diversity and inclusion in the outdoors.*

While she previously worked at a high level as an Assistant Attorney General in the nation's capital, she now lives a nomadic lifestyle in the mountains, and most recently established a base in Cusco in the Peruvian Andes, building a life focused on writing and mountain trekking.

Seth Wolpin *is an associate professor at the University of Washington with a PhD in Nursing, who exemplifies the dirtbag entrepreneurial and philanthropic spirit. Seth is also co-founder of a DIY adventure tour business called Himalayan Adventure Labs and a small nonprofit focused on child education and health in Nepal called Wide Open Vistas. I'm including him as an example of simplicity because, since I've known him, his living situations have included an old RV, a room in his friend's mom's house, and on trails in the Himalayas. Across the years, he's cultivated a life split between a professional career in academics and adventure. He has spent years running, climbing, and fastpacking around the world, and in the process has managed to cull most of his possessions and has avoided picking up more.*

He's a grown-ass man with high-level skills, and I love that at time of writing, he's living out of a metaphorical suitcase with a couple of other professionals-turned-dirtbags who are worthy examples themselves - John Fiddler and Kathleen Egan. They were themselves the subject of this National Geographic article about their shift from career-focused lives into world adventure travelers. They all crash together in Kathleen's mom's house like college kids, but do so in order to simplify their existence to enable ongoing adventure.

Humanism

In Latin America, we encountered the same model multiple times, where local outdoors lovers established guiding businesses to partner with travelers to raise funds for their local communities. In the central highlands of Guatemala, near Lake Atitlan, **Trek for Kids** *operates in partnership with the* **Guatemaya Spanish Academy***, leading hiking tours and taking travelers on backpacking trips to areas that are difficult or impossible to access without a local connection, and all proceeds pay for education for students in communities around the lake.*

And in Sucre, Bolivia, **Condor Trekkers** *provides job training to local guides and raises funds for the communities they hike through in the Andes. They're a concerted partnership between gringos and indigenous Bolivians with a business focus, and they use adventure travel to help locals develop the tools to establish an economic base for themselves in a popular tourist market.*

Chad Guenter*, of Canmore, Canada, founded "Keep Calm and Paddle On" in 2012 as a way to use his love for paddle boarding, and his connections in that community, to make an impact on an issue that was personally important to him - Mental illness. Since* then he's been raising funds and awareness by organizing expeditions and events for SUP boarders, and has been recognized as on of 150 top "Difference Makers" by the Canadian Centre for Addiction and Mental Health.

Troy Nebeker, in Seattle, WA is a similarly motivated paddler who founded a grassroots 24-hour paddling event, "The 24," and the gear brand "Monster and Sea," as ways to raise funds to give directly to families struggling with cancer. The 24 has exploded purely on word of mouth and the hashtag #gobecauseyoucan, to cities around North America. After starting with a modest $7000 fundraising effort in 2015, he was able to donate $140,000 in 2017 to families whose lives were being impacted by cancer.

Another Seattle-based project, **Vertical Generation**, is among the best examples of dirtbags making the world a better place I've encountered anywhere. A volunteer-driven nonprofit that partners with the **International Rescue Committee**, they organize rock climbing courses for refugee children after school, which include mentorship and tutoring to help them keep up with their schoolwork, connect with other kids, learn language and outdoor skills, and develop a sense of community. At a time when the world collectively is treating refugees like shitbags, this volunteer effort fronted by rock climbers is particularly inspiring, and they've received attention from both the New York Times and Outside Magazine for their efforts.

CHAPTER 4: RELATIONSHIPS

Dirtbags, I think, have a genuinely hard time with relationships

The most complicated thing any of us will do in life is figure out how to deal with other people. That's particularly true for those of us pursuing a life that involves doing a bunch of weirdo shit that most people don't understand. If you're someone reading this, prioritizing exploration over your job and basic hygiene, you fit the "weirdo" bill. And I think that's why relationships come up so frequently as a reason that people give up on their dirtbag dreams.

The bad news here is that, if you're looking for specific advice on how to make it work when your husband doesn't want to sell the house to buy a van, or when your girlfriend isn't interested in joining you on that climbing trip in the Alps, I'm afraid I can't provide that. There's just no list of simple rules you can follow that will make all of your relationships work out.

The good news is that, when you really stop to think about it, all the complicated challenges we have to work through in relationships are worth it, because they're one of the main avenues through which stoke spreads in the world.

What do you have to complain about?

People complain about other people. It's the human condition. And to be honest, we're right. Other people can be the worst. We're a bunch of cheating bastards, filthy snitches, and lying assholes who are ruining everything.

But that stuff impacts everyone, and to take a more focused view, when people looking to work more adventure into their life complain about relationships, those aren't the things they are complaining about. At least they're not the complaints that I'm here to address. The complaint I'm here to address is that relationships are major barriers to living out our dreams.

And to drill it down even more specifically, the two biggest complaints, at least in my experience, are that 1) people worry that they'll damage their most important relationships if they really do what they want, and 2) they feel that the important people in their lives hold them back from doing what they want because they just don't "get it," or aren't supportive. Whether it's a concern for leaving behind good buddies, or knowledge that their spouse doesn't like them spending all of that time in the woods, dirtbags often feel like relationships are a major barrier to their dirtbagging.

I don't want to leave behind my friends.

In regards to the first concern, that pursuing your dreams is going to negatively impact some of your most important relationships, I wish I could offer some solace. But actually, my own experience is that it's a justifiable fear.

And, in fact, the most adventurous things we've ever done have also been the most traumatic for our personal relationships.

When we decided, at 23, to move away from our home in the Midwestern U.S. to spend 2 years abroad in New Zealand, it was a major decision that we had no context for. We didn't know anyone who'd made that kind of move, and we were young enough and naive enough that we felt heroic for doing it. It was life-changing in plenty of positive ways.

But there were also a huge number of people who we felt connected to at the time in the Midwest, that we basically haven't seen or talked to since the move. Important people too - friends who were in our wedding, roommates from college, favorite co-workers, and trusted mentors. Take, for instance, my best friend Mike, who I spent most every weekend with as we were growing up. The last conversation we had was a clarification that I was moving to New Zealand, not New England. I haven't seen or talked to him in over a decade. There were no hard feelings - it's just that, when you move across the world, you lose touch with people whether you mean to or not.

Similarly, when we decided to travel for a year and a half starting in 2015, we left a situation where we felt deeply engaged with our local community, and had a tight knit group of friends in Seattle that we'd developed over years and really loved.

Returning back to Seattle after that period of travel, we found that those connections had loosened, and we never felt as deeply attached to the city as we did before we left. Now, as I'm writing, we're midway through selling our condo and moving to a different city. Again - there was no major personal offense that hurt any of our connections. The world just keeps moving, and when your experiences diverge, so do your relationships.

I think it's fair to say that pursuing passions, even when they don't involve travel, can damage relationships. Angel and I have been lucky that our penchant for long hours outside has brought us together, but we've had plenty of friends who've gone through breakups or divorces that were driven not insignificantly by one partner's need to spend as much time in the mountains as possible. Even if you stay close to home, the struggle is real.

Pursuing a passion can damage your connection to your community, create distance in your friendships, or impact your family. It happens. The social cost of a life of adventure is high.

Reality check though: before we get all doom and gloom, or fall into the trap of thinking of ourselves as a particularly beleaguered minority, or start viewing exploration as a particularly problematic passion, loss is the frickin' human condition. The divorce rate in the U.S. is nearly 50%, and everyone I know only keeps up with people from high school because of Facebook. We're not special. Adventurous types aren't the only ones losing relationships because their life paths diverged from the people they felt connected to. Seasons change, people change, and relationships change. Sometimes that sucks, but it's just the way things are.

I don't know if that makes you feel any better, but for me, it's at least encouragement not to fight loss so much. We're all raging against the dying of the light at some level. Loss is a thing to be coped with, not an evil to avoid at all costs. And if loss is going to come anyway, I think that should make you feel a little more free to live your dreams.

My mom won't let me.

I'm not doing a very good job of reassuring you here, because I also think there's some truth to the idea that important people in your life can hold you back from pursuing your adventure passions when they aren't supportive. Parents worry, partners get jealous of your time, friends stop inviting you out on weekends when you always leave at 8 pm to get up at dawn to surf, and kids genuinely need you to devote some energy to raising them. All those dynamics can play in to the decisions you make about how you spend your time.

And just to be clear, that's as it should be. Maintaining important relationships falls into that category of legitimate responsibilities that we talked about in the last chapter that can and should impact what it looks like when you figure out how to live those dirtbag dreams.

It's worth identifying this, and talking about relationships as key responsibilities because - tough love - sometimes we're the assholes.

And there's a particular way that I think we're prone to be the assholes, because it's common to all passionate people who are pursuing counter-cultural values and endeavors. We're prone to bulldoze other people or dismiss them if they don't "get it." If they're not as into it as us, we're at risk of ruining our relationships with them - either intentionally or not - by cutting them off because they don't share our values.

This can be a particularly problematic tendency with the people in our lives who are important to us, and who aren't as stoked on what we're doing as we are. When you're passionate about something that comes with a social or physical cost, it's inevitable that there will be people in your life who wish you could just be normal, or wish you wouldn't take so many risks, or would stay closer to home, or just don't buy it that what you want to do is as important as you think it is. And it's also inevitable that you'll feel some friction in your relationships because of that.

That friction doesn't have to be a bad thing, but it sets us up for a trap, which is beginning to treat those people themselves as barriers. That feels like the kind of "mom won't let me" resentment we all felt as teenagers, and it can be directed at partners, friends, family, and children. And it's toxic for you, and for them.

It's a rule dirtbags: people aren't barriers. They're your partner, your friend, your kid, your relative, or your mom. They're human beings with hopes, dreams, and needs of their own. Just because they aren't as stoked as you are about whatever it is you want to do, it doesn't mean they're a "barrier." It just means that they are different than you. And being different is ok.

Golden Rule: Cool Begets Cool

We've been focusing on the negative because, it's true. Relationships are hard. In many ways, managing relationships is one of the most difficult aspects of living the dirtbag lifestyle. However, it can also be said, that it is one of the most fruitful. There are a few reasons for this.

First of all, having a strong network of like-minded people can be a an incredible resource. Not only is it helpful to have people that are willing to loan you some couch space when you're rolling through their neck of the woods, but these friends can also be some of the best sources of information, inspiration, and support. Where you may face a blank stare when attempting to discuss the intricacies of your newest item of gear with one of those friends or family members that just doesn't "get it," with a fellow dirtbag, you can speak with ease. Here, in the comfort of shared understanding, you can rifle-off jargon to your heart's content. Just scored a sick new GORE-TEX bivy to keep that Western Mountaineering UL 20 dry on overnight stays at the crag? Your dirtbag buddies will know how stoked you are. They get you.

The second major reason to keep your friends close, and your dirtbag friends closer, is that when you surround yourself with cool people doing cool stuff, you are all that more likely to end up doing cool shit yourself. We call this principle, "cool begets cool." It's pretty simple really. You could think about it like this: if you're the type of person trying to make the most out of life, who treasures positivity and optimism, you probably wouldn't want to surround yourself with a bunch of Debbie downers. All that negative energy would just drag you down, right? Well, it's the same when you are looking to live an awesome life of adventure and travel to broaden your horizons. If you devote some time and energy to fostering relationships with rad people, you will open up the doors of near infinite possibilities for rad experiences.

Then of course, there's the whole, "two heads are better than one" concept. I can't tell you how many times I've heard epic stories of adventure, and when asked, "How did you even think to do that?" the response was, "I don't know. We had an idea, then so and so came along, and next thing you know.." The fact is, when a group of like-minded, interesting, ambitious people get together, there's synergy. And so often, this synergy becomes alchemy, transforming an idea that was already pretty gnarly, into something that becomes completely epic and totally unforgettable.

So, although relationships can be hard, I would argue that managing relationships properly is one of the things that makes this lifestyle possible. It is actually at the heart of what we do. Good relationships with the right people can be the fuel that keeps the fire burning, and helps us to do things that are even more exciting than we initially envisioned.

Rugged individualism is a myth.

One popular image of the dirtbag life is the Alexander Supertramp/Chris McCandless model featured in the book and film *Into the Wild*, where the real-life hero set out on his own to brave the wilderness and test his limits. But while the dude did some pretty amazing things, it's important to remember that the story is a cautionary tale, and in the end he dies alone in the woods. Not to discredit any of your personal achievements, but rugged individualism is a made-up game, and the sense that you do anything on our own, without anyone else's assistance, is delusional.

You all are cool, I'm sure of it, but I'm equally sure that you're cool because you've been surrounded by people who showed you the way. And if you accept that, and embrace it, you're going to do even more awesome shit.

You can set out on your own and head into the wild if you want, but I think that fundamentally, the most efficient way to learn to do cool things is to hang around cool people.

Through the process of interaction, there's a churn and a cycle that you can participate in, and when you do, you'll find yourself sucked into things that you never would've initially thought possible.

I'm admittedly speaking mostly out of personal experience here, because every major life experience I look back on and value has been enabled and inspired by other cool people.

Angel had a ton of guts when she decided to travel to Australia, but she was supported and informed by a bunch of people at her university who encouraged her, helped her apply, and helped her figure out how to finance it.

Our move to New Zealand was inspired, to a large degree, by some folks that we met in Australia who had travelled for long periods overseas who made us believe that if they could do it, so could we.

When we decided to start running to get in shape at age 30, the same day we bought our first shoes, we connected with trail runners who gave us the idea to head out into the mountains instead of being bored on pavement.

The idea of thru-hiking only entered our sense of possibility because we met other thru-hikers through the trail running community. And the hike only happened due to help with planning, and support from family and friends.

We got the idea to paddle the Hudson river from a group of paddlers that we met through our business who'd gone on massive, multi-day adventures that sparked our imaginations. Having never done a big trip on water, having these people to help us sort out logistics was absolutely pivotal to the success of our excursion.

So, contrary to the popular image of the outdoors person as a rugged individualist, I would claim that success within the realm of outdoor pursuits hinges to a large degree on the support garnered from others. Speaking personally, I know full well that the main reason that we've been able to do cool things outside, is that we've been lucky enough to be surrounded by cool people.

It comes back to the golden rule: cool begets cool.

Implications of "cool begets cool"

More than any other principle, "cool begets cool" helps provide guidance for navigating the relationship issues that arise when you're trying to center your life on adventure and exploration.

Keeping "cool begets cool" in mind is the antidote for the type of jealousy that arises when you see other people doing cool things that you wish you could. When you stop viewing their accomplishments as a sign of your failure, but rather as a demonstration of what's possible, hearing about things you're jealous of becomes a reminder to surround yourself with people like them - because they're going to show you how it's done, and you're going to get cooler in the process. For example, if your friend runs a hundred mile race, and you look upon that with envy, "cool begets cool" reminds you to buy them a beer and ask them how they did it so you can do it yourself.

"Cool begets cool" also helps you cope - at least retroactively - with the loss of relationships that comes with the dirtbag dream life (or with any life, really). I've talked about how we lost friends when we moved overseas and when we took a bunch of time off to hike and travel. But it's also true that some of our most meaningful and formative relationships have been with people we met in New Zealand and on the Pacific Crest Trail. So although some of our relationships waned a bit, others formed and grew in their place. Through meeting people in our travels, we now have a network of good friends all over the world that continually inspire us (and help us) to do cool shit.

And "cool begets cool" helps you reframe your sense of your role in the community in healthy ways. We've talked about how "people holding you back" is a real thing. But that's a very partial view of things. The actual situation is that you have connections with people who don't understand your passions. Their gift to you is that they have other passions. Your gift to them is that you have passions that they don't. Their cool is different from your cool, and although it can be a challenge to fit these different viewpoints together at times, your job is to keep the cycle of positive interactions going - to take in what they have to say and not reject it, and also to help them see new possibilities by offering up what you are most excited about. Just because you are walking a path that is much different from theirs doesn't mean that you can't still relate. It just means that you need to acknowledge that the dirtbag life can be hard to understand, especially for those still firmly conditioned in the status quo. The lesson here, is that if you flaunt your coolness, you will probably be seen as an asshole. If you can embrace humility, and realize that other people may not fully understand (at least yet) the meaning of your lifestyle, you can share your passions with them in a way that may be inspiring, or even catalyzing. Who knows? You may even be the spark that lights a fire in them to start thinking more about what they really want in life. Heck, maybe they'll even hop on the dirtbag train at some point. But this will only happen if you inspire them. Not if you insult or infuriate them.

So with this, comes the understanding that "cool begets cool" is also a responsibility. Being cool means *not* being an asshole. If you are fortunate enough to be out there doing super cool shit all the time, then you have the responsibility to be a positive role model for others who may be looking up to you for inspiration on how they can bring more cool into their lives. Be proud. Be in love with your life. Embrace and cherish your role as a dirtbag. But don't be a dick, because that's not being cool.

Romance

When you want an adventurous life, it stands to reason that you want an adventurous partner, and the dirtbag ideal is to find someone that is going to be both a romantic fit *and* an adventure buddy. It's rare, but sometimes it happens, which I can attest to because Angel and I (at the time of writing), have been together for 20 years and married for 16. Together, we have navigated numerous stages of life, and a variety of epic experiences.

It's worked, in large part, because we're lucky, and both a little bit codependent. But also because "cool begets cool" has been in full effect, and, despite the fact that we have significantly different personalities and ways of tackling the world, we've figured out how to learn from each other.

The other key, is that we've learned how to work *with* each other. Looking back at all the crazy things we've done - from rambling through Central America, to navigating the Hudson on kayaks held together with Gorilla Tape - I can recognize a pattern in how these trips came to be. While you might think that these adventures were born of shared inspiration and mutual consensus, in reality, it's typically been more of the opposite. Generally, it has been that one of us has come up with some ridiculous (yet intriguing) idea, then works tirelessly to talk the other into it.

Frankly, usually Angel is the one with the ridiculous ideas (and I'm the one who has to be talked into it), but at various times, the process has gone both ways. We've already talked about the Australia trip, which I was initially completely dubious about. Angel also talked me into the idea of moving abroad after college, but to my credit I was the one who sold her on New Zealand. We took up running, which eventually lead into trails and ultras, after we watched an Ironman on TV and Angel suggested that she wanted to do that (we never did, exactly, because swimming's hard). We'd planned to hike the Camino together with friends, but I talked her into running it. She brought up the idea of quitting our jobs to hike the PCT (which I really didn't want to do initially), but she eventually sold me on it. And after we bought a couple of folding kayaks, I came up with the idea to take them across the country and paddle them down the Hudson.

All of this worked out for a couple of reasons - beyond just the fact that both of us have a shared interest in adventure. First, both of us are relatively flexible people. We've both been open to trying out most of the things that the other person has been interested in, even if it meant a bit of compromise for one of us. So it hasn't just been about finding the perfect fit - it's been about being flexible enough to adjust when needed.

Second, perhaps most importantly, our success has come from mutual respect. We have our issues, but at heart, I think both Angel and I really respect each other. We see strengths in the other person that we want to learn from, because they complement our own weaknesses. In important ways, we both want to be more like the other person, and that keeps us pushing forward as a unit.

It hasn't always been easy, but by learning how to work with each other we have been able to do a lot of fun stuff that we likely would not have done without the inspiration and support of the other person, teaching us that having the right relationship partner can be a huge asset to living a badass life. It's an intimate and very special expression of "cool begets cool."

So the pragmatic takeaway from all of this, which I think is universally applicable in relationships, is that you should really only be with someone who you respect, and who respects you. Whatever your interests, don't waste your time in relationships with partners who don't respect you, and if you don't respect your partner, check yourself, because you're likely developing an unhealthy relationship.

What if my partner doesn't like to go outside?

You could say that one of the reasons why Angel and I experience a lower degree of difficulty in our relationship is because we have passions that, for the most part, are fundamentally compatible. Although (as stated above) we have learned how to work with each other on the specifics, our general passions are shared ones: we both love travel, adventure, and being outside. It's fairly obvious that if both partners are dirtbags, living a dirtbaggy life shouldn't be all that hard. But what happens when one partner has an all-consuming passion for the outdoors, and the other doesn't?

While I've been lucky to not experience this first-hand (thanks honey!), I have seen many instances of this in friends and colleagues. But fear not! Even if you're reading this from your tent while your partner is cuddled up at home, you can still have both and awesome relationship *and* a rad, outdoorsy life. The key, once again, is mutual respect.

Our friends, Tom and Jessica Kelley, are a great example of this. Jessica is a ridiculous adventure badass, who, as I'm writing, is on a multi-week, 1,350 mile combined bikepacking and packrafting solo expedition in the Yukon - which is basically just par for the course for her. Tom likes to make booze, and has a distillery in the suburbs of Seattle. In a lot of ways their passions don't seem to have much overlap, but the dynamic in their relationship, at least from an outside perspective, has been one of serious mutual support. Tom is frequently providing logistical support for Jess's adventures. Jess is frequently pushing Tom's products and has supported him in turning a passion project into an actual business. Even if they haven't participated a whole lot in each other's passion, they've enabled it. Cool has begotten cool.

And in a similar way, our friends Will and Jennifer Thomas have enabled each other to do amazing things in totally different arenas. By training, Will is a real estate guy, but by passion he is a trail runner of the most extreme sort. When he's not out completing some of the hardest races in the country (including the Hardrock 100, an elite race in the San Juan range in Colorado that's seen as a pinnacle challenge in American trail running), he'll be found somewhere up in the Cascades on one of his many solo, overnight, off trail peakbagging adventures. Jennifer, by contrast, is a professional classical musician who spends a good deal of her time practicing or performing with other notable musicians throughout the country. A few years back, they decided that Will would quit his job to support Jennifer's career, which in the meantime freed up flexibility for Will to take on outdoor projects that wouldn't have worked with a traditional schedule. They've figured out how to make potentially conflicting life paths function in complementary ways, because of mutual respect.

Friends

Do people typically view friend relationships as difficult to navigate? I don't know. The reason I feel like I need to say something about them here, is that they've been another important place where I've experienced the "cool begets cool" principle in action.

There really is a deep truth here: to meet cool people, you have to decide to do cool things. But to do cool things, you need to know some cool people. In my experience, when you make the call to do something, and start telling other people about it, like-minded people are going to latch-on and help you get there. Taking the first step is really all that's needed to get the cycle going.

Our path towards ultra-running, for instance, started almost immediately upon deciding to take up running at all - through some degree of luck, but also because of the circles that running put us into contact with. We didn't realize it at the time, but we bought our first pairs of running shoes in Seattle at a store started and run by trail running legends, and even though our first run out the door was only 12 minutes long (we bought pastries to celebrate afterwards) the seed to check out local trails was planted by a trail run that we saw advertised the first time we were there.

It was on a trail run led by the owner of that store that I met another guy (my friend Adam) who was running ultras and training for a 100. During a subsequent random encounter at a bar, he invited me to pace him at the end of his race. It was during that pacing experience that the possibility of running a 100 myself first entered my head. When I ended up running the next year, Adam paced me.

And through the same community of trail runners, we were introduced to the idea of thru-hiking the Pacific Crest Trail. It was really only after hearing our friends' passionate talk about the experience that we decided to take it on ourselves. Once we announced our plans to do the trail, our experienced friends jumped in to give us the information and logistics we needed to complete it successfully.

Friends have put us up on their couches, given us free beta, paced us in ultras, supported long adventure runs, helped us get a business off the ground, and will probably make up the lion's share of early readers of this book. I have to give friends a shout out. Whatever our individual flaws, the outdoor community is a bunch of interesting people hanging out together, and pushing each other forward to keep the "cool begets cool" cycle going.

I think relationships with your friends and family are like romantic relationships in that they only work when they are characterized by mutual respect and reciprocity, so don't be jerks to each other, and don't feel obligated to hang out with people who are jerks to you. But the main thing is that when we're all in this together, we can do some cool shit.

Kids

Kids though! Kids are definitely a challenge!

For a lot of people, kids are the antithesis of the dirtbag dream. Dirtbagging = the freedom of the wild. Kids = the shackles of the suburbs. When those of us without kids think about having them, we assume that it will require that we quit doing fun stuff in order to make sure they don't die or end up weird.

There's truth in the idea that having a child is the ultimate in legitimate responsibilities, and that it makes it more complicated to just run off into the woods whenever you want to. Kids require money, time, attention, and focus, and they're people with their own interests and needs that might not line-up with yours.

It's also true that one can make a solid moral argument against having children. There are plenty of people in the world. Some say that the world is already facing issues stemming from overpopulation. It may be a biological instinct to reproduce, but it's not a necessity or obligation. People who don't want kids shouldn't feel like they are bad people if they don't have them. It is just as selfish to have children to meet your own emotional needs as to *not* have children to follow your dreams.

All that's true.

But I also think that it's a bit silly to think that children are incompatible with a life built around adventure and exploration. Maybe I'm getting old, but I want to build a durable philosophy of life here, and I can't espouse an approach that suggests that having kids can't be a part of the good life. Bringing children into the picture might make things a bit more complicated, but it doesn't make it impossible. Becoming a dirtbag raising dirtbag kids just requires a bit more creativity and dedication to the cause.

Cool parents beget cool kids

I think this brings us back to our first principle, because the reality check for those of us who poo poo the idea of raising children while also living a non-traditional lifestyle is that your relationship with your children is the ultimate venue for the "cool begets cool" dynamic.

After all, in real life, no adult really cares that much about emulating you. They might be happy to crib some lessons from your experience, but we all have our own issues to deal with and our own pride in ourselves, and don't generally need heroes and role models.

But your kids! Until they turn into teenagers and start wanting to punch you, your kids care about *nothing* more than impressing you, learning from you, and being like you. Against all evidence, they think their parents are the smartest, strongest and most impressive people in the world. It's weird but true.

And because of that, parenting is the ultimate opportunity to put the "cool begets cool" principle into practice by providing direct opportunities to expose children to life's myriad possibilities. Kids make their own decisions, but as a parent, you are the one who will largely determine if they are going to have the opportunity to live their lives adventurously, and provide a model for what that will look like. More than anyone else, you're their dirtbag role model, and have the most powerful opportunity possible to be an ambassador for the things you love.

So, the older I get (and the more I see my cool friends

spawning), the more I think that the idea of conflict between an adventurous lifestyle and parenthood is more about a lack of vision than any actual conflict between the two.

I'm not a parent, so I'm not going to offer a ton of advice, because what do I know? But, I am a nurse who specializes in pediatric psychiatry, so I can give a professional opinion that there's nothing inherent to the dirtbag life that prevents one from becoming a good parent. Kids do have some basic needs, but they can be met in a variety of ways. Along with food, water, and shelter, in order to be healthy, kids need an unconditionally loving family, confidence in their own abilities, peers and other people to play with and learn from, safety and security, and the type of discipline and structure that gives them a sense of the rules of life. But all of those things can be provided in most any living context. Getting kids outside with you, and sharing what you love with them, I'd argue, can be a great avenue to cover all of those bases.

And like a lot of things, when you accept that there is more than one way to do things, you start to see really interesting examples that change the narrative around parenting.

When we were on the Camino, we met a family with a toddler and an infant walking across both France and Spain with a donkey. By the time we met them, they were three quarters of the way there, and their kids were having a great time.

Our friends Ras and Kathy Vaughan raised their daughter in an off-grid shack, working odd jobs in the summer and spending winters at the ski field. Their daughter is awesome now, a college graduate in her early 20's who has already spent two years in Madagascar with the Peace Corps and is now traveling the world.

And in fact, when I think about it, the kids I've met with adventurous parents have all turned out super cool themselves.

Angel and I saw this kid named Andrew Miller running a series of ultras in the Pacific Northwest with his parents and brother through his teenage years, and people consistently questioned whether or not it was problematic. Then, in 2016, he won the most competitive trail ultra in the country - the Western States 100.

We also know a mom, Amy Martin, who pulled off hiking 1600 miles of the Appalachian trail with her four children in 2013, two of whom were six and one of whom had Down Syndrome. All of those kids are freaking amazing now. Between the group, they are doing things like living abroad, competing internationally in the Special Olympics, professionally acting, and writing plays. And you can't help but think that their exposure and immersion in adventure was related - those kids have a perspective on life's possibilities far beyond my own when I was a dorky 16 year old trying to sort out what to do with my life.

I'm not a parent myself, but from the outside it seems like parenting is like everything we've been talking about here. When you see possibilities rather than freak out about limitations, you can do cool things. Cool will beget cool, and there are plenty of kids living out amazing experiences as a core of their upbringing. If you want kids, you can feel free to raise them doing the same.

In Conclusion...

If I had to make a concluding statement on relationships (and it appears that I do, or else this chapter wouldn't fit the introduction/body/conclusion model that nonfiction readers have come to expect), it would be that, yeah, if you want to buy a van and live in it for six months of the year, or take seasonal work at ski hills, or raise your kids in a yurt in the Montana backcountry, there are going to be some relational challenges. Some people aren't going to be willing to go along with you on that.

But the most important story to tell about relationships in the outdoor community is that cool begets cool. The community sucks you in, if you let it, because it's a big mass of people who are doing inspiring, fun, creative things, and by participating in that churn, you learn to do inspiring, fun, creative things yourself. And you enter into a cycle where you contribute back to the community by helping other people do the same.

So don't fret about relationships. If you're committed to living your dreams, just look forward to all the cool people you're going to meet, and the unexpected things you're going to do as a result.

Doing Better than Ed Abbey

"Cool begets cool" is a purely optimistic principle, and I admit that I'm pushing it, in part, as a counterpoint and corrective discourse to problematic trends in dirtbag culture.

You can't really be immersed in outdoor culture and talk about relationships honestly without recognizing that there is some seriously messed up shit going on here, just like everywhere else. We're as baseline homophobic, transphobic, racist, and xenophobic as any other group.

But we also have our own particular issues. Climbing and hiking cultures have a reputation for misogyny and bigotry. I've experienced the thru-hiker creep thing, and have heard of plenty of female hikers having to move faster to get away from guys trying aggressively to get into their pants. A quick Google will net plenty of examples of rape culture and bigotry in outdoor culture.

My point isn't to malign the dead, but I think it's helpful to consider one of our archetypes because it helps point to particularly problematic dynamics in dirtbag culture as a whole.

Ed Abbey was in many ways the quintessential Dirtbag hero. He was maybe the founding philosopher behind radical environmentalism, which he promoted out of a deep love for nature that he wrote about beautifully. He wrote two of the most influential dirtbag works - "Desert Solitaire" and "The Monkey Wrench Gang" - and he has been a key archetype for Dirtbag counterculture due to his iconoclasm and his "retreat into the wilderness for as long as you can and only come back when you have to" approach to life. When he died, his body was hauled in a pickup to a hidden grave in the desert to avoid the inhumanity of modern medical intervention. The image he created of himself was a poetic representation of an alternative way of being that re-centered wilderness and the human connection to the world we live in.

But he also was, in just as many ways, a toxic asshole. In perhaps his most definitive biography, "Adventures with Ed," the author (Abbey's best friend, Jack Loeffler), portrayed him as a serial philanderer who cheated on all five of his wives and ignored his children through much of his life. In his own words, Abbey was an unrepentant bigot and xenophobe.

From his "Confessions of a Barbarian"

> "Am I a racist? I guess I am. I certainly do not wish to live in a society dominated by blacks, or Mexicans, or Orientals. Look at Africa, at Mexico, at Asia."

> Garrett Hardin compares our situation to an overcrowded lifeboat in a sea of drowning bodies. If we take more aboard, the boat will be swamped and we'll all go under. Militarize our borders. The lifeboat is listing."

As the second paragraph suggests, Abbey justified his essential anti-humanism with an environmentalist veneer - keep more people out because they'll destroy what we have - and the author he quotes wrote the book "The Tragedy of the Commons", which is about the way that the collective action of self-interested individuals undermines the success of the whole.

But an asshole with environmentalist justifications is still an asshole.

The reason I think it's worth considering Abbey's example isn't about him

I think there's a story that's told in the outdoor community, reflected in Abbey's archetype, where being a dirtbag means retreating to the wilderness to get away from people, fending them off when they try to invade the wilderness you so value. It's fundamentally an "us vs them" story, and is ultimately narcissistic. In that type of environmentalism, there's an assumed sort of anti-humanism, where other people are viewed primarily as a part of the problem.

In Abbey's case, I think that this sort of anti-humanism also was incorporated into the story that the closer you are to nature, the less you will concern yourself with regulating your baser instincts towards other humans. As if being a virile, natural human means leaving your instincts towards treating other people like shit unregulated. So philandering and racism are natural outcomes of a life of freedom in the wilderness. Maybe not positive, but an understandable expression of the human being in its natural state.

My instinct is that this type of attitude is an undercurrent in much of the outdoor community, and it manifests in toleration of the type of misogyny and sexual harassment that we unfortunately bear witness to in the culture more broadly. In too many other cases, we see discrimination in the form of thinly veiled racism. This isn't about Abbey - it's about a spirit that he exemplified that is present in the outdoor community as a whole.

I think we can do better than this. Humanism vs environmentalism isn't a zero sum game, and the attitude that being a virile, natural human means leaving your base impulses unregulated is juvenile - not countercultural or iconoclastic. And the idea that the way to protect what you have is to keep other people from accessing it is self-centered and unrealistic - not a workable solution.

It's not a panacea, but this is a reason I think it's worthwhile to argue for a positive, humanist posture as we're building this dirtbag community.

While the dirtbag retreating to the wilderness to protect themselves from the marauding masses is one story, the more predominant one, in my experience, is "cool begets cool." Dirtbags who are out there meeting other people doing cool things learn to do these cool things themselves. Then by doing so, they are able to inspire other people to do the same. This creates a positive feedback loop in which people learn to help other people. This is a pattern that can be seen as much in the ski bum or thru-hiking communities as it can within the circles of environmental activists. At its core, it's fundamentally pro-human and anti-chauvinism of any kind.

So the community that I'm interested in building - and that I think will be the healthiest expression of what dirtbags can bring to the world - is one where humanism stands alongside environmentalism due to the recognition that "cool begets cool."

.

CHAPTER 5: FINDING MEANING

The "Golden Rules" we've covered so far offer a grand outline of an alternative way of being. We eschew the pursuit of money to "go further with less" to maximize the amount of adventure we can experience in our lives. We put our careers in their place as a means to an end, secondary to our vocations of exploration and adventure. We reject mainstream definitions and adopt our own set of rules about what it means to be responsible human beings. And we immerse ourselves in the cycle of "cool begets cool" as our guiding principle for navigating relationships.

I would guess that this has been in the background of your thoughts, but at some point in all of this you have to ask yourself the question, "why?" Why the hell would you live like this? Why does any of this matter, or make sense? Why take a risk, throw away a chance at a good career and a normal life, to go stink up a tent in Potrero Chico?

While for some people, the initial draw might be escapism or romance, for the people who embrace the outdoors as a lifestyle, ultimately it sticks because they find it *meaningful*.

What I mean when I talk about meaning.

The idea of asking questions about "meaning" may smack of religion, or raise the suspicion that I'm trying to indoctrinate you into some kind of weird dirtbag cult.

While that might be a good money making strategy, it's not the point. I'm not raising questions about the grand design for dirtbags or the divine mandate to quit your job and buy a Vanagon. I'm not here to offer any hidden spiritual truths, or sell you any snake oil.

So to be clear about what I mean when I talk about meaning: I'm not talking about something esoteric or philosophical. I'm talking about the concrete emotional experience of living on a day-to-day basis with the feeling that you're doing what you should be doing, and that the life you're living is worthwhile.

I'm talking about it for entirely practical reasons. So many people dive into some dirtbag pursuit, driven for a variety of reasons to try out a life that seems exciting and romantic, but burn out and quit. For many, the dirtbag dream is a phase that only lasts as long as they're still having fun.

Worse, for others, the type of peripatetic, exploration-driven lifestyle we're talking about can be a trap that they never figure out how to escape. The ski bum who drinks and skis, not because it's awesome, but because they can't figure out anything else to do with their life is a real, sad thing. *National Geographic* even wrote a depressing article about it a few years back, and research has documented an increased suicide rate in outdoor towns.

So, in order to prevent that - either burning out or descending into hopelessness - we have to talk about how dirtbagging can be a path towards a meaningful life.

My story

In some ways, it was inevitable that we'd end up here, in this type of conversation, because my outdoor adventure experience has been steeped in my own ongoing struggle to maintain a concrete feeling that what I'm doing in life is worthwhile. I'm a bit of a melancholy depressive at baseline, and my life, since adolescence anyway, has seemed like an ongoing midlife crisis. For me, the outdoors has been a salvation.

But my story is a little bit complicated, because the sense of meaning that I've found in various outdoor pursuits has ebbed and flowed. At times it's worked, at times it hasn't.

While I've always liked the outdoors at some level, it was around my 30th birthday that I began to find deeper meaning in my time spent there. The more I began to sooth my existential woes in the sanctity of the woods, the more my outdoor pursuits began to take the shape of a lifestyle more than a pastime.

I started running at 30 ostensibly to "get in shape," but the real reason I kept doing it was because it became therapy. At the time, I was going through a process of quitting my first career path as an Episcopal minister, and leaving behind religion all together. I'd lost my means of making an income, burned bridges with friends and family, and generally stepped into a void without knowing where I'd end up on the other side. In short, life felt out of control and meaningless.

Running felt both like a thing I could control, and a way to offset negative emotions through the flood of endorphins that it produced. And the experience of progressing from the couch to the finish line of a marathon (and ultimately ultramarathons), provided a positive offset for the negatives in my life. I may have felt like I wasted 10 years of life. My friends may have hated me. And I damn sure may have been feeling terrible about myself. But I could run a hundred miles, and that had to mean something. And when I was running, none of the other stuff seemed to matter anyway.

After about five years with a single-minded focus on running, with dozens of ultras and weekend adventures under my belt, the motivation to keep doing it started to wane. I liked the activity, and the experience of going into the wilderness regularly, but I just didn't have the intense, natural drive to keep going further.

Looking for the next step, thru-hiking seemed like an appropriate choice, in that it offered a new set of challenges that would serve as a powerful stimulus for personal growth. Perhaps, it would also provide even more meaning to my life as an adventurer and athlete. After ultras, the question of whether I could walk 2650 miles though the wilderness on the Pacific Crest Trail was intriguing. What would it be like? How would it change me? If trail running was a way that life could feel meaningful on the weekends when we were at home, would thru-hiking be a way to have that experience full time?

Unfortunately that original attraction faded dramatically when my father was diagnosed with an aggressive form of brain cancer, and died midway through our PCT thru-hike. We left the trail to be there when he died, and the experience triggered a complicated wave of emotions - starting initially with pain and anger, but then settling in to an obstinate and overwhelming sense that life was meaningless.

We got back on trail after he passed, and finishing the second half of the hike became a way to protest against that sense of meaninglessness. It was a way to assert that I was going to keep going; I would take advantage of life, no matter how much time I had. It was also a way to put trust in the things I knew made things feel better - the outdoors, and hard work.

It wasn't a solution, and I vacillated between numb or angry for much of the two months that it took to finish the hike, but on the whole, it helped.

While some people experience thru-hiking as a calling, once we finished I never wanted to do it again (perhaps due to the negative emotions associated with our experience). And I didn't really want to go back to ultra running either. We'd hit our max on long days on trail, at least for a while.

Not that that meant a retreat back to the work-a-day world. Actually, quite the contrary. After the PCT, and our ramblings all through the American West, we continued our adventures with a full-on vagabond odyssey in Latin America - an extension of the impulse to keep moving that became so ingrained in us while thru-hiking. It also served as an opportunity to continue to push back against the sense that life was meaningless. It was a way to do things I was scared of, and had dreamed about. And it was a way to have experiences that I knew I would regret missing out on if I didn't pursue them. There was still a lot of pain in the experience, but it felt like raging against the dying of the light.

Eventually with that as well, I hit a point of burnout. The outdoors and travel were things I had been able to mine in order to create meaning - as avenues for personal improvement, or therapy, or symbolic progress in the face of loss. But by the end of the year and a half that followed my dad's death, it stopped working. The dirtbag dream of traveling and hiking in some of the most beautiful areas of Patagonia, Bolivia, and Peru felt like just wandering around looking at pretty things - not some grand adventure.

And so, again, we pivoted - we learned a lot along the way, centered on the experiences we had in the outdoor community, and the idea that you can live a great life without much money. We returned to our home base in Seattle, went back to work, and started to develop ways that we could reconnect and play a meaningful role within the outdoor community at large.

The result of our ponderings on that topic was the idea to start our own company, *Boldly Went.* We're still doing the stuff we love outside, but less frequently, because the motivating mission has shifted from participating *in* the outdoor community, to working towards contributing *to* it. What our experiences have taught us, is that this community, and the incredible experiences that it fosters, has tremendous value. We have come to believe in what it has to offer the world, and feel like we have something worthwhile to contribute to it. And in that way, we've been able to re-establish a sense of meaning that is perhaps more potent than ever.

Golden Rule: To keep going, make it meaningful

Maybe it's my own experience with the outdoors as a place where lives are changed, or the fact that I'm approaching a stage of life when people normally struggle to figure out what the hell they're doing with their lives. Whatever the case, I think this final bit of dirtbag advice is the most important I can give: To keep going, make it meaningful. There's an excitement and sense of adventure that drives us to pursue a life lived in the wilderness or off the beaten path, but it's that sense of meaning - the sense that we're doing what we're made for - that allows us to sustain this type of life in the long term.

Because "feeling like your life is meaningful" can be such an esoteric idea and ephemeral experience, I want to be as practical and concrete as I can in this discussion, so in order to talk about this, I've turned to resources from science, and particularly from the study of human psychology, rather than spiritual or philosophical sources.

I tend to view "a sense of meaning" as a concrete emotional experience that can be cultivated and developed with practice - similar to the way that physical health can be cultivated with exercise and diet, and financial health can be cultivated with saving and discipline.

And I think that the challenge for the dirtbag is that in living an unconventional life, they opt out of the traditional avenues through which most of our peers cultivate a sense of meaning - career progression, established deep roots in a particular location, financial and material accumulation. So we have to come up with our own strategies.

Luckily, the core activities of the dirtbag life, as we've been discussing, can provide a sure path towards a meaningful life. That's what the rest of this chapter is about.

One of the most influential recent thinkers on the topic of cultivating meaning is an author named Emily Esfahani Smith. She's not a "spiritual leader" or guru, but a journalist with a Masters in Psychology who is interested in the question, and has interviewed a diverse group of people about their answers. She congealed her research into a book, *The Power of Meaning: Crafting a Life that Matters*, and in order to organize our conversation, we'll use some of the core concepts from her research, as they are relevant to your life as someone who longs to drift off into the wild.

In the series of interviews she conducted, she identified four concepts that people repeatedly identify when they talk about what gives their life meaning. We'll structure the rest of this chapter to talk about the ways that the type of lifestyle we've been outlining here - centered on adventure and the outdoors - addresses all of those themes.

Her four themes are:

a) Purpose
b) Belonging
c) Transcendence
d) Storytelling

Purpose

While the terms "purpose" and "meaning" are sometimes used synonymously, in this discussion, purpose is different from meaning in that it essentially means *making yourself useful*. That can mean having a "cause" - politically or religiously - but it more generally means having a sense that what you're doing is valuable to society. Having a "purpose" means having a sense that your life isn't being wasted, and that you're making concrete contributions to the world.

While the general "recreation" model of outdoor adventure can imply that dirtbagging is essentially self-indulgent, my argument is that it can provide a sense of purpose, because it *is* useful.

Sometimes that usefulness is personal. As both trail running and thru-hiking did for me during especially difficult life transitions, the outdoors can provide free therapy, or lead to personal growth. While those are things that are self-focused, they aren't self-indulgent. The purpose of diving into surfing, climbing, hiking, or trail running isn't necessarily hedonistic. It's "Starting with the man in the mirror" to quote that famous weirdo.

Sometimes the usefulness of outdoor recreation is to provide an outlet so we can keep going on to other things that matter. Even the Mockingjay had to retreat into the woods in the districts from time to time during her war with the Capitol. Recreation itself is an essential part of human existence, and creates balance with action. Author and activist Terry Tempest Williams hit on this concept in her book, *The Hour of Land* when she said "Wilderness is not my leisure or my recreation. It is my sanity."

I shit on Ed Abbey a bit in the last chapter because he was an asshole, but one of his best known quotations gets right to the heart of this sentiment:

> One final paragraph of advice: do not burn yourselves out. Be as I am - a reluctant enthusiast....a part-time crusader, a half-hearted fanatic. Save the other half of yourselves and your lives for pleasure and adventure. It is not enough to fight for the land; it is even more important to enjoy it. While you can. While it's still here. So get out there and hunt and fish and mess around with your friends, ramble out yonder and explore the

forests, climb the mountains, bag the peaks, run the rivers, breathe deep of that yet sweet and lucid air, sit quietly for a while and contemplate the precious stillness, the lovely, mysterious, and awesome space. Enjoy yourselves, keep your brain in your head and your head firmly attached to the body, the body active and alive, and I promise you this much; I promise you this one sweet victory over our enemies, over those desk-bound men and women with their hearts in a safe deposit box, and their eyes hypnotized by desk calculators. I promise you this; You will outlive the bastards.

At other times, playing outside leads to making yourself useful in other ways. As Yvon Chouinard said, and as we discussed in the chapter on responsibility, when you spend your whole life in a place, you feel responsible for it. When you feel responsible for it, you act. That can mean utilizing your skills to tackle issues related to the outdoors, and it can mean using your connections in the outdoor community, or the things you've learned there, to improve the world around you.

Whether it's through improving the outdoor community itself, fighting for the environment that we're a part of, or finding a cause to balance with your recreation time, the outdoors provides avenues for purpose.

Belonging

Esfahani Smith's second concept, Belonging, means having strong relationships with other people that are defined by a shared sense of mutual value. You're connected with people you like who make you feel like you matter.

While the outdoor community might have started out, roughly, as a bunch of weirdos spending too much time doing fringe activities, now it is fertile ground for these kinds of relationships for a huge number of people.

I personally experienced this during the period when I was transitioning out of religion and into the outdoors lifestyle, and the trail running community essentially replaced my previous community. The dynamic I noticed was that the nature of the activity lent itself to quick, tight, meaningful bonds. Long days of risky, strenuous activity lend themselves to close relationships because of the forced reliance it fosters, and the sense of shared struggle. Climbing, mountaineering, thru-hiking, surfing, paddling - all are hard, sometimes dangerous things that you do with other people. In concrete ways, if you belay someone on a climb, or assist someone in a wilderness rescue, you matter to them. Nothing bonds like shared struggle, and that creates a quick and strong sense of connection within a community.

As dirtbag culture has developed, I would argue that it has gotten a lot of its energy from a similar sense of shared struggle. The subculture is an alternative way of existing, and figuring that shit out requires close connections with other people who are doing the same. Reshaping our careers and relationships, rejecting common social values - that is hard work. We need each other. It's why there's energy in this book - the attempt to define the community we're a part of, and what we're about.

Transcendence

The third thing that Esfahani Smith says is essential to a

meaningful life is a sense of transcendence.

Like with the term "meaning," transcendence might seem like an esoteric concept - the kind of thing Gwyneth Paltrow would use to try to sell you eye cream or something. But in fact, it is a relatively concrete experience that I believe is familiar to most people in the outdoor community.

"Transcendence," defined clearly, means having a sense that you are a part of something greater than yourself. The important thing is not that you can convince yourself that this is true at a cognitive level, but that you actually *feel* that way emotionally on a regular basis. It's like the difference between believing that your partner loves you when they tell you, and *feeling* it when they go out of their way to make you happy. Transcendence is the emotional experience of being a part of a big, overwhelming, beautiful universe.

Dirtbag, and world-class climber Alex Honnold has talked about this. When asked by his National Geographic interviewer Simon Worrall about whether he "experiences God" in high places, he replied:

> Um, definitely not. [Laughs] I'm quite the atheist. But I have probably experienced some of the same emotions that people associate with spirituality: the feeling of oneness with the world and the sense of awe and wonder and our own smallness, which religious people equate with some kind of higher power or god.

For me, the outdoors has always been the most important avenue to create those sorts of feelings. I've come to some of my most important epiphanies during long walks on the coast where looking across a vast expanse of water produced a sense of the bigness of the world that calmed my anxieties and put me into a deeply reflective state.

Skiers, bikers, paddlers and runners sometimes talk about experiencing "flow," which Lance Hickey described in an article on the topic from *Huffington Post* as "moments in which your mind becomes so entirely absorbed in the activity that you "forget yourself" and begin to act effortlessly, with a heightened sense of awareness of the here and now." Flow is found in skiing turns effortlessly and instinctually, or losing hours of time on the trail without thinking about pain or the effort of moving: this is also an experience of transcendence - of moving outside of yourself into something bigger, not physically, but emotionally.

Outdoor activities are day-in, day-out reliable means to experience life as meaningful because of the feelings that they produce. Playing outside is what keeps us sane, what changes negative feelings into productive ones, and what reminds us that we are a part of something bigger than ourselves - even if it's not always clear what that is. For the outdoor community, they're our disciplines and our rituals - the way we stay connected to that amorphous transcendence, however we define it.

Storytelling

The final thing Esfahani Smith talks about as providing a sense of meaning is storytelling.

I personally didn't understand this one when I initially read it, but now, it makes a lot of sense.

In order to have a sense that your life is meaningful, you have to be able to construct a coherent story about your life. You have to be able to define where you came from, how you got here, and why, as well as where you are headed in the future.

Storytelling is related to the point about transcendence, because if transcendence is the emotional experience of being a part of something bigger, having a sense of our own story is the way that we get our minds around that cognitively. It's how we tell ourselves who we are, and why we matter, and integrate ourselves into the world in a way that makes sense.

This observation is a great place to finish our discussion in this book, because to a large part, making sense of our collective story is what this whole thing has been about.

As human animals in the grand scheme of evolution, we're the few whose environment and peculiar genetic makeup has driven us to follow our instincts towards exploration. For some that's because of a driving sense that things suck, and that there has to be a better world somewhere. For others, it's the inherent desire to ferret out new possibilities for ourselves, and for the people around us.

In the course of human history, we are part of an ongoing tradition of explorers, vagabonds and nomads who have set out into the unknown to see what is over the next ridge, down the river, or across the ocean. Our type has played the role throughout history - for better or worse - of landing humans in previously uninhabited spots, and creating churn in the gene pool and world politics.

In our current social situation, we're a counter culture developing a critique of some specific shitty realities of modern life. The world needs us, and we're doing what we can to chart a better path.

You'll have to figure out where you fit in to all of this yourself, but in my opinion, as individuals, we're people trying to stay sane in a crazy world. Rather than accepting the hand we've been dealt, we're doing our best to figure out how to live a good life - an amazing, adventurous life - by stretching the resources we have as far as they can possibly go. We're people committed to playing outside not just for fun - but because it matters; because being fully human means being intimately acquainted with the dirt, fire and water from whence we came, and to which we'll all eventually return.

Conclusion

If I can conclude on a bit of a sermon, I want to encourage you to protect your sense of meaning - and don't let anyone tell you you're wasting your time.

The outdoors is an avenue to a regular connection with a larger reality.

The world is eternally screwed up, and it needs critiques of the dominant paradigms that aren't working.

The environment is being damaged every day and it needs people who are sticking their nose in the polluted places for fun, and pointing out that our oceans are made of plastic and our mountain tops are gone because of the strip mines.

Humanity is capable of destroying itself - whether at the hands of a reality show clown president or a rogue state nuclear power. It needs people wandering between cultures reminding us that we're all in this together whether we like it or not.

Technology is pushing humanity further and further from the

memory of what it is, letting us sink deeper into our illusion that we're anything but a bunch of monkeys intent on convincing the other animals we're not. The world needs people in touch with their humanity, their mortality, and place in the natural world.

And for a million reasons, the world needs people who know how to have a good time for the hell of it. People who want to run through the hills because it's breathtaking and swim in the cold ocean because it makes them feel alive. People that push their limits because it provides a good buzz and who aren't afraid to sail through a storm because it makes for a good story later.

So protect that sense of meaning - the world needs you.

CONCLUSION

Dirtbag, hiker trash, beach bum, ski bum, vagabond, rail meat... There's a pejorative term for every expression of this impulse to spend life exploring outdoors. If you've made it this far with me, I hope it's because we've come to a shared agreement that these monikers should be embraced with pride.

Pursuing a life spent powder chasing, thru-hiking, or world travelling is a beautiful, worthwhile existence, not just for your own self-actualization, but for humanity as a whole. Dirtbags are part of a proud explorer's tradition, as well as a burgeoning counterculture that provides needed correctives for some of the most dehumanizing excesses of modern existence. Plus, it's just fun.

People talk about "living your dreams" like it's magic or rocket science or something, but we're really just talking about cutting out the crap you don't care about and devoting your time and money to the things that you want to do. And I hope that, if nothing else, I've given you at least a little bit of confidence that this lifestyle we're talking about is genuinely *possible*. We're not just a community of elite athletes and trust fund vanlifers. We're also not just a community of irresponsible misfits. Dirtbags are all that stuff, but we're also normal people who happened to decide at some point to figure out a way to pursue the modest goal of sleeping with our heads in the dirt more nights than not.

Your dirtbag dreams are going to look different from mine, or anyone else's, but if you follow the Golden Rules, you'll figure out how to get there, and do it in a way that you'll be proud of. Pragmatic, responsible, beautiful dreamers are what you dirtbags are, and what we're carving out together is a lifestyle - not just a commitment to our particular sport.

Going further with less is a great short-term strategy for making a particular adventure happen, but it's also a philosophy on life that keeps us from getting wrapped up in meaningless material pursuits.

Accepting exploration as a vocation, and career as a separate consideration, doesn't have to devalue your career, or discount the possibility of making money doing what you love. But it does lead you to embrace an important truth: you're more than your job, and in fact your job is just a means to an end. It's dirtbag wisdom that the world could use.

Honing your sense of "responsibility" may seem problematic to people you'll encounter along the way, but it doesn't mean rejecting obligations altogether. It means adopting wholeheartedly the idea that your calling to explore is *itself* a sacred responsibility which, when practiced properly, will both make you a better person and the world a better place.

Embracing the "cool begets cool" principle in your relationships puts the focus in the right place: on using relationships to make a positive contribution to the world while also getting better at what you love.

And living this dirtbag dream, in all of its facets, will provide you with a path towards the elemental goal that humans have pursued throughout history - a meaningful life.

What we've done here has been both practical and theoretical, and it's been an attempt to do something new - to offer a comprehensive explanation of what it means to be a dirtbag. We've outlined our definitive values (Exploration! Going Outside! Being a cheap-ass! Not buying into the BS! Spending our lives doing cool shit!), as well as our pragmatic strategies for hitting those goals. This probably won't be the last word on the subject, but I hope it's an interesting start.

I'm a basic dude, and I'm not convinced there's much genius here, but that's really the point. Angel and I have been able to put together a life filled with incredible experiences outside, because we've spent a lot of time figuring out how to center exploration and avoid wasting time and money on things that don't matter. We've done it as normal people with normal backgrounds with average incomes and levels of ability. There's a good chance that, if you're reading this, you already *want* your life to center on your passions outside. I hope this little ramble has made you feel like that's an entirely possible life strategy that can be pursued in a variety of ways.

My own final piece of advice (the most important rule, really), is that there's no right or wrong place to start. The only wrong way to live a life of adventure is *not* to. So as a final exhortation, whatever else you do, get the hell out there and have some fun!

Sleep outside on a work night. Hitchhike across a state. Move somewhere you don't speak the language. Get a job on a boat and sail across an ocean. Spend too much time playing outside.

Ski bum for a season or hang out in climber camps for a summer. Swim in questionable water. Walk across your city. Bandit camp. Join the Peace Corps. Paddle to the middle of a lake before work. Stink until you stop noticing it. Live off of other people's detritus for a while. Sleep on a friend's couch until you start to feel self-conscious. Thru-hike.

Whatever the means, experience for yourself what it feels like to explore, to sacrifice, to suffer, and to be human, and do it with the terrible knowledge that others might not, and that they may need you to give them the courage to follow their path.

In the end, you're all going to die, so live a life that feels like it means something.

APPENDIX

If you had a good time here, I hope you'll check out our website at www.BoldlyWentAdventures.com to subscribe to email updates, listen to the podcast, check out live events, read more of what we write on the blog, and get notifications about upcoming books. And I hope you'll check out our Patreon page (Patreon.com/boldlywent) to become a supporter and get free stuff we only share with our BFFs.

We've covered a lot of ground here, and I don't want you to have to dig back through to find the websites or books I've recommended, so here they are, divided conveniently by category, with some other favorites thrown in for good measure.

All of these resources are accessible online – usually for free, occasionally for purchase. I haven't included the full web address, except where absolutely essential, because that would have been outrageous. Just type the references into Google and you'll get there!

In case you're wondering, I don't get any kickbacks from any of these - I just think they're great resources, and I consulted them while writing this book.

Dirtbag History and Culture

- Yvon Chouinard, *Let my People Go Surfing.*
- *Wild Defined*: "Are you a Dirtbag? A growing social movement." by Candice Burt
- *Cipher Magazine,* "Because We're Insane" by Sara Fleming,
- *Backpacker Magazine,* "A Ghost Among Us" by Megan Michelson

On Ed Abbey:

- *New York Times*, "A Friend, Not a Role Model: Remembering Edward Abbey, Who Loved Words, Women, Beer, and the Desert," by Blaine Harden.
- *Utne Reader,* "Was Edward Abbey Racist and Sexist?" by Keith Goetzman

General strategies to be cheap

Strategies for travelling on as little as $10/day:

- *Nomadic Matt* profiles Tomislav from Croatia: https://www.nomadicmatt.com/travel-blogs/travel-ultra-cheap-interview/
- Matt Kepnes, *How to Travel the World on $50 a Day or Less*

Travel Hacking: Strategies to fly for free using points and airline miles.

- Matt Kepnes, *The Ultimate Guide to Travel Hacking*
- Chris Guillebeau: *Travel Hacking Resources*

Jobs and Careers

Get a coach to help you make big moves.
- Rob Zimmerman, *FindYourInnerCompass.com*

General Advice:
- *The Barefoot Nomad,* "45 Great Jobs You Can Do While Traveling the World and How to Get Them" by Micki Kosman

Hostel/Backpackers
- HostelJobs.net
- Workaway.info
- helpx.net

Organic Farming
- wwoof.net

Flexible or non-traditional work schedules
- flexjobs.com

Cool Jobs
- JobMonkey.com
- Backroads.com
- Cooljobs.com
- Coolworks.com

US National Park Jobs
- www.nps.gov/aboutus/workwithus.htm

For Digital Nomads
- Remote OK
- WeWorkRemotely
- Indeed
- Fiverr
- Upwork

Side Hustles
- Chris Guillebeau's *Side Hustle School*

- *Desk to Dirtbag's* "Adventure Calculator" for determining how much adventure your Side Hustle will finance.
- *Desk to Dirtbag,* "42 Ideas for Side Hustles"

Health and Travel Insurance

- Healthcare.gov
- World Nomads: Travel insurance specifically covering adventure sports.

Other reliable travel insurers:.

- Atlas
- Allianz
- IMGlobal

Eat for Free

- Freegan.info
- robgreenfield.tv/dumpsterdiving

Ride for Free

- Stick your thumb out
- Pop Rideshare
- Craigslist.com
- rdvouz.com

Sleep for Free

- Specifically for people who are bike touring: Warmshowers.com
- Couchsurfing.com

- Freecampsites.net
- Campendium.com

House Sitting

- Trustedhousesitters.com
- Mindmyhouse.com
- Caretaker.org

Long-term Financial Strategies:

- Matt and Julie Urbanski, Urbyville.com
- *GoCurryCracker.com*
- *OurNextLife.com*
- Steph Davis' "Dirtbag Financial Plan"
- *Investopedia* on "Paying Yourself First"
- Vicki Robin and Joe Dominguez, *Your Money or Your Life*
- *Desk to Dirtbag*, "Conquering Debt Mountain"
- *Desk to Dirtbag*, "On Financial Independence and Investment"

Free Financial advice

- SmartAsset.com
- Nerdwallet.com

Resources for Developing a responsible dirtbag culture

Women, Trans, and Gender non-conforming climbers
- Alpenglowcollective.co
African-Americans, People of Color, and the Outdoors
- Outdoorafro.com

- Girltrek.com
- Vertical Generation
- Refuge Outdoor Festival
- *Reno Gazette Journal,* "For People of Color, Hiking Isn't Always an Escape", by Benjamin Spillman

Ethical and Sustainable Travel

- Peak Explorations (Marinel de Jesus, aka Brown Gal Trekker)
- Climbing South America
- TemporaryProvisions.com
- EthicalTraveler.org
- Wide Open Vistas (Nepal)
- Himalayan Adventure Labs (Nepal)
- Condor Trekkers (Bolivia)
- Trek for Kids (Guatemala)

Environmentalism

- Erica Prather, The Sacred Rage Podcast

Water Protection

- The Ikkatsu Project

Fundraising for families dealing with cancer

- The 24
- Monster and Sea

Living like a human in an inhuman world

- UltraPedestrian.com

On the makeup of the outdoor community

- *The Outdoor Industry Foundation,* "The Shape of our Community: Outdoor Foundation Research Reports"

Misogyny in outdoor culture

- *Outside Magazine,* "Hostile Environment," by Krista Langlois

Mental Health and outdoor culture

- *National Geographic,* "Here's Why Ski Towns are Seeing More Suicides," by Kelley McMillan

- Keep Calm and Paddle On

Microadventures/Loving your local outdoors

- *Alastairhumphreys.com*

Relationships

- *Dear Sugars Podcast:* Cheryl Strayed is taking questions directly.

Being adventurous with kids

- *Outside Magazine,:* "Notes from the Child-Full Life" by Katie Arnold
- *Duct Tape then Beer*, "The Next Chapter: Dirtbag Parenting" by Lindsay DeFrates
- *Oars.com,* "10 of the Best Websites for Adventurous Families" by Kimberly Tate
- *Backpacker Magazine's "how to raise a backpacker"* tag

Discovering the meaning of life

- Emily Esfahani Smith, *The Power of Meaning*

ABOUT THE AUTHOR

Tim Mathis is a graduate of the Pacific Crest Trail, El Camino de Santiago, and the Cascade Crest Classic 100 Mile Endurance Run, among other things. He has contributed to *Trail Runner Magazine, Grit City Magazine,* and *UltraPedestrian.com,* and with his wife Angel, he is the co-creator of the *Boldly Went* podcast and event series, where outdoorists of all kinds gather to share their adventure stories with their neighbors and the world. This is his third book.

Made in the USA
Columbia, SC
20 April 2019